HOW TO BE A
STUDY
NINJA

STUDY SMARTER   FOCUS BETTER   ACHIEVE MORE

GRAHAM ALLCOTT

ICON

Previously published in the UK and USA in 2015
under the title *How to be a Knowledge Ninja*
by Icon Books Ltd, Omnibus Business Centre,
39–41 North Road, London N7 9DP
email: info@iconbooks.com
www.iconbooks.com

This edition published in the UK and USA in 2017 by Icon Books Ltd

Sold in the UK, Europe and Asia
by Faber & Faber Ltd, Bloomsbury House,
74–77 Great Russell Street,
London WC1B 3DA or their agents

Distributed in the UK, Europe and Asia
by Grantham Book Services,
Trent Road, Grantham NG31 7XQ

Distributed in the USA
by Publishers Group West,
1700 Fourth Street, Berkeley, CA 94710

Distributed in Australia and New Zealand
by Allen & Unwin Pty Ltd,
PO Box 8500, 83 Alexander Street,
Crows Nest, NSW 2065

Distributed in Canada by
Publishers Group Canada,
76 Stafford Street, Unit 300,
Toronto, Ontario M6J 2S1

Distributed in South Africa by
Jonathan Ball, Office B4, The District,
41 Sir Lowry Road, Woodstock 7925

Distributed in India by Penguin Books India,
7th Floor, Infinity Tower – C, DLF Cyber City,
Gurgaon 122002, Haryana

ISBN: 978-178578-237-4

Typeset in Myriad Pro by Marie Doherty

Printed and bound in the UK by Clays Ltd, St Ives plc

To Roscoe. This one's for you, chief

CONTENTS

1. THE WAY OF
THE STUDY NINJA

The alarm goes off. Your brain slowly remembers that it's not the first time you've heard that alarm this morning. You look at the time. 'I can't have snoozed for *that* long, surely?!' It's Wednesday. You have an assignment due tomorrow. Time is running out and this morning's planned extra hour of reading just became an extra hour in bed, which isn't an ideal start. Oh, and you're probably going to miss the bus now and be late for the start of the class.

You shouldn't have gone out last night. Your friend just said to come round for dinner, but then dinner turned into the whole night. You feel tired and foggy and not quite ready to face the world. As you look at the texts on your phone you remember that you said yes to an extra shift at work tomorrow night (well, you do need the money), but with another deadline looming on Monday, it's going to be a busy few days ahead. A crazy few days. In fact, you already know that these next few days will look nothing like the peaceful and serene plan you created for tackling this term, just a few short weeks ago.

'Why don't things work out like I planned?'

'Why do I always find myself in a mess?'

'Juggling all these things is so damn *hard.*'

These issues are what this book is all about. It's about helping you move from muddling through to becoming a Study Ninja – slaying the enemies of stress, chaos, procrastination and feeling overwhelmed, and creating a sense of playful control and momentum in all that you do.

It's easy to feel like everyone else has cracked it and that you're the only one in a mess. So I'll let you into a little secret – everyone feels like this. From the most powerful business leaders and politicians to the coolest people on TV to your friends, family and role models – they're ultimately all human beings with their struggles and faults. As human beings we're more prone to mistakes than we like to think: we plan badly, we're not realistic, we're not organized enough to have a good enough view of what's ahead, we struggle with prioritization, we get scared and nervous and oh, how we wish there was an exam for procrastination, because we'd be guaranteed an 'A' for that one (although we'd probably put off that exam until tomorrow, come to think of it!).

That's part of the problem with creating study plans or reading study guides – life isn't perfect and we forget that *we're* not perfect either. We keep finding ourselves in a mess because life is … *messy*. Yet study books and our own grandiose plans sell us the dream of perfection and we fall for it every time. We dream about this perfect life we can lead and convince ourselves that buying a smart new notebook and some highlighter pens is but the first step on our inevitable journey to awesomeness. Three weeks into the term, those dreams have faded again and we're back to feeling disappointed, flustered, daunted and messy again.

How do I know this? Well, I've spent the last six years coaching and training senior business leaders in how to be productive and successful, and I wrote a bestseller that helps people do that in their work and life, called *How to be a Productivity Ninja*.

And how did that become my job? Because I was spectacularly *bad* at productivity. Because I tried to live the perfection myth too. Because I'm naturally flaky, lazy and disorganized. Because I'd struggled so hard at making myself productive that I found it easy to relate to other people struggling and could help them find solutions.

I was far from a grade 'A' student. You should see my school reports. Oh wait, my mum still has them in her loft. And now I'm reading them again after all these years, they're even less pretty than I remember them. And I have even less of an idea about why she might choose to keep them …

'Graham's mark here is about average but does not reveal the number of reminders that have been necessary before work appeared'
—Mr Abyss, Chemistry

'Graham is still satisfied with inaccurate work in his writing. He continues to rush his homework'
—Mrs Bettany, French

SUBJECT REPORT

HISTORY

Lawrence Sheriff School

Name: *Graham Allcot*

Form: *11?*

Grade: *11?*

Dated: *21/11/86*

Exam:

It is the same old story – Graham can work well in class – but not out of school hours. He is only hampering his own chances of doing well. If he wishes to do well – the power and effort must be his.

'It's the same old story –
Graham can work well in
class, but not out of school'
—Mr Cartwright, History

TUTOR REPORTS

Lawrence Sheriff School

Name: *G Allcot*

Form: *11?*

Form Tutor:

Dated: *27.3.95*

Headteacher: *I.A. Goodes*

'Incapable of simply arriving
on time in the morning, I am
not surprised at his present
problems with coursework'
—Mr Goodes, form tutor

'The progress he has made has been
pulled out of him, and most credit
for it goes to others, not himself. He
sees it as a little local difficulty, but
his attitude to organized study is
in fact a major future problem'
—Dr Rex Pogson, Headteacher

What those reports don't tell you is that I was learning loads in those school years, but very little of it was in school. I was editing a music magazine, singing in a band, campaigning for political change, putting on music events, writing a music column for my local newspaper, DJing on a local radio station, as well as delivering newspapers six days a week and working in a bank three evenings a week. But I still look back on some of those school years as a wasted opportunity. If I'd have known what I know now about topics like productivity, attention, psychology, self-control and motivation, my school days – and my qualifications – would have been very different.

Since those days, I've learned something really important about learning itself, too. Knowledge is power – it's a cliché because it's true. But we've come to see education as a passport to a better pay packet, and as a 'chore' that's necessary for us to reach the next level in life, when really we should see it as a path to a richer life experience. Yes, there's a destination to reach, but why not make the journey richer, more fulfilling and more interesting, too?

This mindset shift happened for me when I was studying for my degree, at the University of Birmingham's famous and pioneering Centre for Cultural Studies and Sociology, set on a beautiful campus in a fascinating multi-cultural city – home of course to the Balti curry, Tolkien, Cadbury's chocolate and, of course, Aston Villa Football Club.

At the end of those three years, I was given a degree and I was happy that within weeks of graduating, I got a job doing something that I cared deeply about. Conventional wisdom is often for people to abandon the thought of education or personal development at this point. Why would you need to keep learning when you've reached the pot of gold at the end of the rainbow? But the thing that university gave me – that was much more important than the piece of paper I could use to inflate my salary expectations – was a deep sense of curiosity, a thirst for knowledge and understanding about how the world works, and excitement at finding out what makes people tick, what principles or politics are worth fighting for, how the world and society should develop. I'd finally learned that there is nothing as exciting as asking big questions, knowing full well that you're unlikely to get a simple answer.

So, dear reader, whether you're studying for your GCSEs or A-levels, your degree, or your French class after work, my hope is that this book ignites within you a passion for learning as well as giving you skills, techniques, tips and tricks from the world of business and productivity that mean you can take your learning to a new level. If there's a destination you have in mind – a qualification, a life stage, an achievement – then I would be delighted to be your guide on that journey, and I promise we'll get you there in good shape.

But my aim will be to go further: my real aim will be to give you the gift of playful curiosity that my three years studying at the University of Birmingham gave me. Whether you're learning for school, for college or university or just for the fun of learning, my intention here is to show you the way.

You have a reason for wanting to learn. Perhaps it's to make your parents happy, perhaps it's to advance a career or perhaps it's for the sheer unadulterated pleasure of learning new things. It could be a combination of all of the above, or something else entirely. But let's be honest, there's also plenty of reasons not to learn, too. It could be that amazing new series on Netflix, it could be the distraction of the football scores or the Xbox, it could be your family or a great book. All of these are enemies of progress, because you're human. As much as we all like to feel we're above such distraction, and as much as we beat ourselves up at our regular lapses into spectacular bouts of procrastination, it happens. We're human. We know it's not good for us. We do it anyway.

For the past decade or so, I've been obsessed with productivity. I became obsessed with it because I was fed up of watching myself fall for bad habits, struggling to find ways of being organized and in control and realizing the sheer inefficiency of so many of my approaches to work and life. Ever since I started my company, Think Productive, and started teaching productivity at some of the best-known companies in the world, one of the most common things people have said to me is: 'I wish they taught these kinds of skills in schools.'

I quite agree: I was lousy in school. I had no awareness of how to study well, I struggled to hold my attention on things for long enough to do great work (by the way, this never changed, I just developed better ways around this!) and I never really felt I hit a groove until well into my degree – and only then because I felt so totally engaged and inspired by the subject matter, which I'm realistic enough to know is a luxury in itself.

What wins on a rainy Tuesday? Is it the passion to study hard and get ready for those exams or assignments that we know have gloriously far-away deadlines that feel like some kind of distant island on the horizon? Or is it laziness, distractions and socializing?

Do you want to change this so you can be more disciplined, memorize facts better, develop critical thinking skills and write better essays? Of course you

'Get over the idea that only children should spend their time in study. Be a student so long as you still have something to learn, and this will mean all your life'
—Henry. L. Doherty

do. So how do you change all this and more? You learn to think like a Ninja, harnessing nine key characteristics that will focus your mind and revolutionize your learning.

HOW TO USE THIS BOOK

This book is split into three main sections. First, we will focus on creating the mindset and habits that are conducive to studying: the way of the Study Ninja, mental approaches to your studies that will have you seeking out the shortcuts, maximizing your learning time and feeling more in control and less chaotic. We'll look at what it means to be a learner and discover the style of learning that suits you. Essentially, the aim of this section is to prime your brain to receive and retain knowledge in the most efficient way possible, and remove some of the obstacles to doing so.

Then in the middle chapters, we'll use this newfound Study Ninja mindset to approach the key tenets of learning, playing to your particular learning styles and strengths: general study, note-taking, group work, writing, revision and exams.

Finally, we'll look at a subject that is close to many a student heart – reducing procrastination. But I want to also focus on what we can replace procrastination with: increased momentum, overcoming your fears and developing a childish curiosity that will make learning fun and help you learn for the rest of your life.

It's a book that I hope you will choose to read cover to cover, but I know that you may not have time for that! So before we get started, if you've picked up this book in a panic, over on the next page there's a map so that you can cut straight to the chase, whatever today's chase may be.

'*I AM SO STUPID!*'

We've all uttered those words as we look back with regret on the times we wasted and look forward at the deadline hurtling towards us at startling velocity, ready to smack us in the face. We wasted time and now we're rushing. How stupid of us. Do you ever wish you could just turn back the clock, rewind all those hours of TV and movies and games that in hindsight were pretty pointless (though fun!)? The temptations we face are what make us human. We can't simply decide one day to become a superhero, immune to such distractions and such sloppy and lazy working practices. But we *can* learn to think like a Ninja. Ninjas are human beings with a great mindset, good tools and the ability to overachieve. And let's face it, everyone loves a Ninja.

So here are the nine characteristics of the Study Ninja. All of these things can be learned with a little practice. They are ways to approach your learning, ways to think about the world around you, ways to promote your own self-discipline and banish some of the negative habits that keep you feeling down. So, my Ninja apprentice, let's dive right in.

BALANCE

THE NINE CHARACTERISTICS OF THE STUDY NINJA

1. BALANCE

A Ninja needs balance in their life. Learning is just one of many priorities. It might not be your top priority and striking the balance is about fitting in the learning so that you have time for the things that truly matter. Alternatively learning might be the thing you most want to do, but life is getting in the way.

JUGGLING

The older you get, or the deeper you get into your studies, the more potential there is for 'everyday life' to get in the way. It can be overwhelming. Making space for studying or writing is half the battle. Feeling good about it is the other half! There are several ways in which approaches to productivity and learning are similar, not least in terms of building structures and 'scaffolding' that enable you to juggle everything going on in your life without getting overwhelmed or forgetful.

'Scaffolding' consists of the structures and systems that you need to have in place to engender good habits and to feel in control of your decision-making. Developing a great to-do list so that you know what your options are and don't feel stressed by all of those nagging things to do is one of the most important things you can do to alleviate stress. A great to-do list becomes like a second brain: a brain that's actually better than your real brain, because once things are written down, it doesn't forget them.

Getting into great routines requires more than just having the thought that it would be good to have a routine! To change your habits and develop great routines that stick, you need to think about the scaffolding again. Do you keep meaning to check your email or get round to that big chunk of reading, but it never happens? Do you keep telling yourself you need to be making progress on that essay, yet you're watching Netflix instead? Those are not just problems of willpower or decisions, those are problems of scaffolding! So later in this book we'll be focussing on self-management techniques that will leave you procrastinating less and doing more.

RELATIONSHIPS

'I can't break up with her this week, she's got her A-level exam on Thursday.' We've all heard sentences like that uttered by friends, or even said them ourselves! Relationships take time to nurture and offer another powerful pull away from study. Whether it's the early days of lust and love, the relationship with a parent or sibling or a strong friendship, these things really matter. There is also a lot made of the concept of 'work/life balance', and if you're studying for a qualification, it can often feel like you have no study/life balance. And if, like I did all the way from the age of fourteen to the end of my degree, you're studying alongside trying to have a life AND holding down a part-time paid job, it can often be a big challenge. Work/life balance implies two things, when in reality we're all juggling three, four, five or more major areas of commitment in our lives.

SOCIALIZING

And of course alongside all the serious stuff that requires your commitment and focus, there's the *even more* serious stuff like drinking, dancing and cavorting, especially if you're at uni. Some schools or universities will try to set limits on how much their students should be socializing, but I don't know that I've ever met a student of any age or institution that has been keen to obey such rules. In fact, it seems to me that this only encourages more socializing in order to achieve a requisite level of rebellion. And of course, if you're a mature student, with a social life spent well-away from a campus, or prefer to spend your relaxation time doing other things, such guidelines seem even more alienating. There's also peer pressure at play here – we want to feel accepted and avoid the 'FOMO' feeling (fear of missing out).

In addition to having a life outside of the campus and outside of your own four walls, we all have a life online. This is often more complicated and 'bitty' than the socialising we might do on a designated night out. In fact, it's often so second nature these days that we even forget that it's happening or that we can do something about it! But think about how much time you spend on your phone, or on the internet. Personally I know there are times when I need to make sure I've switched this stuff off and got it out of the way. But equally, there are times when a few minutes of social media diversion can be a healthy thing that leaves me feeling refreshed for a task – and other times when a full-on Facebook binge beats going out too!

To study successfully, you don't need to abandon the idea of socializing. In fact, there are academic studies that suggest socializing actually helps with the retention of key information. But there are times to strike the balance, and in particular, we'll look at the 'cross-over' between the two. For example, scheduling in revision study time the morning after a big night out when you're tired and not at your best is very unlikely to lead to academic prizes, yet we kid ourselves that such behaviour strikes a good balance. But actually, being prepared to write off the whole of Sunday in advance is one of the most sure-fire ways to enjoy your Saturday night without guilt. So let's be real about the best approaches to achieving balance, rather than falling for the pretences that make us feel virtuous, but that, if we're honest, are very rarely effective.

BACKGROUNDS AND SPOTLIGHTS

How we deal with Balance has a lot to do with where we choose to put our attention and focus (more of which later!). One of the best ways to achieve a sense of Balance is 'backgrounding'. Learning to push things into the background until we're ready to shine the spotlight back on them is an important skill. So there are times when relationships take centre stage, and times when we should 'maintain' them with the least possible effort. There are times to hit the socializing hard and times to put it to the background. More subtle things, like the 'life maintenance' of bills, shopping or fixing things can easily feel like they need constant spotlight, yet they're things that often need some 'backgrounding' if you're going to really focus on what matters.

BALANCE COMES FROM PURPOSE

Finally, let's start with the biggest question of all: why?

Why do you study? What are you learning *for*? What's your intention? I often think that starting with the big, profound question of 'why' and really thinking about what's motivating you is an inspiring and empowering thing to do. As a culture, we're not encouraged to be curious or question things – in fact, I would even go so far as to argue that, wrapped up with all the learning, education in this country often deliberately attempts to brainwash us never to question our assumptions or intentions.

We're taught to go to school, get good grades, follow an academic path or get training, get a job, get a pay rise, buy a house, have children, retire and go on a cruise ship around the Caribbean … And perhaps achieving all of those things, in that order, *is* exactly why you're learning. But it's almost certainly not. You might just enjoy being clever and smart. If so, admit it! In my case, a big motivation behind wanting to go to university was because I would be the first person from my family to go, and having been to a ridiculously good school where it was an expectation, I felt confident about breaking the mould. And once I got to university, I was learning because I wanted to be like the academics in my department who had their words published in journals and even in the *Guardian* newspaper. And they liked drinking grown-up coffees and wore badly fitted cardigans and it all just seemed quite romantic. Yes, the motivation for many of the hours spent in the university library was dreaming that one day I too could wear ill-fitting knitwear.

I know this sounds like I'm asking you to think about the meaning of your life (and in a way I am), but I do think it's important to know at least some of the reasons you feel that learning is important to you. After all, you do have choices. You could put this book down, quit your course and spend the rest of your life deliberately learning nothing.

I'd like you to think now about what it is that drives you. What's it all for? Is it really about getting good grades, or do the grades matter because they make your mum smile, or contribute to a bigger life plan of yours? Take a few minutes to figure it out.

EXERCISE: PURPOSE

Write down the reasons you really want to study, and why you want to get better at it below:

I am learning because I want to …

1. _____

2. _____

3. _____

4. _____

5. _____

I want to be a Study Ninja because …

1. _____

2. _____

3. _____

4. _____

5. _____

ZEN-LIKE CALM

2. ZEN-LIKE CALM

A Ninja is calm, present and 'in the moment'. OK, a quick warning. Things are about to get a little bit 'hippy'. But stay with me here, because the first secret of success is coming your way here.

You will often hear people say they work at their best when they're on a tight deadline. They feel like the deadline makes them more productive. This is a half-truth. The deadline forces you to get going and make progress. And in those final hours before the deadline, as you struggle to get everything finished, you have no decisions to make about what you should be spending your time on. You stop thinking about Facebook updates or gossip websites or football scores as you work away, blissfully in the moment. In the middle of the panic of that deadline is a calmness, because all choice has been removed. There isn't the time anymore to procrastinate or even work on something else: meeting the deadline and working like a Trojan to get there requires all of your attention.

It's not the deadline itself that makes you productive, it's that feeling of being totally focussed on that moment. Time stands still. You forget the worries of your life; you might forget to eat; you might even struggle to remember what day of the week it is. This is a version of what Buddhists call 'Zen'.

We spend so much of our lives living in anything but the present moment. We plan our futures, we strive for pots of gold at the end of the rainbow instead of marvelling at the rainbow itself, we agonize over bad choices we might have made, or mourn things that we've lost. And with our work, we spend so much time in the planning that we let our imaginations run wild thinking about the negative impact of bad work, bad grades or bad decisions. Such worry gets us nowhere. In fact, it causes paralysis.

So our aim as a Study Ninja is Zen-like Calm – to reach a state where we're interacting only with our intention, in the present moment.

Having strived for and practised this for a number of years now, I can tell you it's very possible to have the Zen-like Calm bit, without the stress and worry of the deadline.

GETTING INTO THE ZONE, GETTING INTO THE ZEN

Getting into the 'work zone' doesn't happen by accident. TV on in the background? Turn it off. Music on in the background? Only if it's something that you know you don't have to think about (personally, jazz and electronic music work for me whereas any music with a strong chorus or a lot of words like rap doesn't, because it tempts me to think about the words or sing along). Are you surrounded by piles of unrelated books? Move them. Make your desk or workspace a sanctuary. And yes, you know that connection you have to all the information in the world, ever? The internet connection on your computer or phone? You might even want to spend some time closing all those windows and apps – these are all enemies of the present moment, enemies of Zen-like Calm.

THE BRAIN AND THE BODY

The second issue to consider on your quest for Zen-like Calm is your physical well-being. Is your body rising and falling with fixes of coffee or caffeine-heavy energy drinks? Are you eating brain foods like fish and nutritious fresh vegetables, or are you gorging on fast food? And are you getting some level of exercise? Unfortunately, this does actually matter! All of these things affect how the brain works. In fact, look at heat map studies of brain activity after just fifteen minutes of exercise versus those of people who stumble like zombies to their desks in the morning, and it's really no wonder that Richard Branson starts every day in the gym (and has even said that his morning workouts are the secret to his business success). So getting the physical right gets the mental right. It makes it easier for the brain to think clearly, it gives you a better quality of attention and it aids learning.

STRESSING ABOUT YOUR STRESS

We all face stress. Stress is a natural physiological response to something that threatens or challenges us. To some extent stress can actually be a good thing, in that it can provide motivation or a sense of urgency. But it's also the enemy of Zen-like Calm: stress can motivate you to get started, but too much stress will leave you stuttering, distracted and unable to learn effectively. So being mindful of stress – and more specifically what kind of stress has your attention – will allow you to overcome it and develop that Zen-like Calm. We will talk later in the book about attention management techniques (because it is attention management, not 'time management', that we need to worry about) and we'll talk procrastination, fear and how to leave them far behind you when you sit down at your desk. The Study Ninja knows that battling stress is one of the hardest yet most profound things you can learn to do – and something that affects not just your ability to learn, but your ability to live, too.

RUTHLESSNESS

3. RUTHLESSNESS

As well as fostering Zen-like Calm, a Ninja is Ruthless. Ruthlessness doesn't mean cheating or being unethical, but we do need to be much bolder in how we deal with ourselves and with others. In particular, we need to be ruthless with how we protect the most precious resource that we have: our attention. Attention is a variable resource, which is a fancy way of saying that there are times in the day when you're on top of your game and other times when you feel tired, sluggish or unable to think clearly. Scheduling your work for the times of day where you know your attention is strong is not something that we're ever taught, or something that comes naturally to most of us. We'll talk more about this later on and focus on self-control, too. But for now, a few key elements to think through:

THE ART OF SAYING NO TO YOURSELF

It's often said that 'sorry' is the hardest word. But really 'no' is harder still. Ever heard the phrase, 'It's easier to apologize than to ask permission'? It's saying that sometimes you just need to ruthlessly crack on with something that furthers your cause, even if you know it might annoy people. 'Sorry' is easy to say if you've ended up getting what you want! But how about saying 'no' to yourself? Your favourite team are playing this evening and it's live on TV. Yet you have an important assignment you need to complete this evening, too, and if you don't start it until after the game finishes, you'll be tired and flagging before you get anywhere near the end. Sometimes we just need to say no to ourselves.

We're living in a world in which delayed gratification is becoming as alien as sending paper letters. We have the tools at our fingertips to buy anything we want, watch anything we want, speak to anyone at any time (no matter where they might be in the world), learn anything we want, go anywhere we want … So why wait? Well, because delayed gratification and the art of saying no to ourselves is one of the secrets of successful people: entrepreneurs start and run businesses knowing that it takes an average of three years for a business to become successful enough to make them any real money (I can attest to this personally!), and in that time a lot of people abandon their businesses because they run out of patience. Develop the ability to delay your gratification and keep going – knowing that good things come to those who wait.

SAYING NO TO DISTRACTIONS

So you just need to be ruthless with yourself, right? Wrong! Some of the biggest distractions don't come from us but from other people. If you're studying alongside having any kind of a life (and let's face it, that means pretty much everyone), then being ruthless in managing what else you allow to have your attention means occasionally saying no to some really flattering or exciting things. Do you need to be on that committee? Do you need to go to that big party? Do you need to take on more hours with your job? It's important to create some space in your life to truly commit to your learning. If you don't do this, and just pretend you can fit it in, you'll end up spreading yourself too thinly and not making anyone happy.

How do I know this? You want to know my guilty secret? I do this. All the time. At school doing my A-level exams, I was on the school council, lead singer of a band, learning guitar, working three nights a week in a bank, involved in political campaigns, a DJ on the local radio station, writing and editing a music fanzine and holding down a relationship. These days I'm exhausted even reading that list out. And while I loved almost every minute of every one of those things, in hindsight they damaged my learning and it's no wonder I had to take a year out and resit one of my subjects to get into the university I wanted. Am I better at this now? A little. But my optimism and passion to make things happen often blinds me to this particular weakness. I've started businesses I had no time to run, committed time to charity projects when I've had important work deadlines and for many years the result was working weekends and evenings. These days I work a strict four-day week and employ an assistant to help me as a bit of a 'gate-keeper'. I'm a lot more ruthless with what gets my attention. But could I be even more so? Yes, of course. Being a Ninja is always a work in progress.

PLUG IN, UNPLUG, TUNE OUT

The Study Ninja needs to protect their attention from distractions. There are all kinds of ways to do this, but one of the best is being mindful of your relationship with the internet. Did you know that your computer and even your home internet connection has an 'off' switch?! Well, use it. Take some time to turn your phone onto silent, put it in a drawer and relinquish your connectedness, just briefly. An hour of Zen-like focus, away from distractions, is a truly powerful thing.

Perfection is the enemy of done. The last moments you spend on something are rarely the best ones. Being Ruthless means learning to 'ship' – to release what you've created out into the world before you're comfortable doing so. Software makers know this all too well. They don't wait for something to be perfect, they just wait until it's good enough. The near-perfect software that the developer is still working on isn't a product at all, it's an idea in someone's head and on a screen. Perfectionism is a disease because it tells us to hold onto whatever it is we're doing until it's perfect, and that until something is perfect, it's unfinished. Yet in order to balance and juggle our studies with our lives, in order to make space for everything that truly matters, we need to learn to be comfortable with 'good enough'. Of course, if your life consisted of simply one study assignment, you'd probably keep working on that one thing for ever and ever until it was utterly perfect, until the person marking it could give it no less than 100%. But the problem with this thinking is that in reality you have another three assignments to prepare for, more reading to do, a whole world of ideas to explore, a job, a family and a life.

There's a principle we'll look at later called the Pareto principle, which says that you get 80% of your results from 20% of the effort and time. That doesn't mean only spending 20% of the time you thought you might on particular tasks, but it's worth using that principle to focus not on the 'time in' but on the 'impact out'. Focussing on what you want to achieve and working backwards is a great way to reduce inefficiency and get more Ruthless with your attention.

WEAPON-SAVVY

4. WEAPON-SAVVY

A Ninja needs to be Weapon-savvy. There are a wealth of tools and resources at our disposal as we seek to be organized, use our attention productively and learn effectively. These break down into a few different types:

▶ **Thinking tools.** These are general rules and principles to follow, and ways to arrange our thoughts. Mind-mapping is a good example of a thinking tool; once you learn how to do this, it can really help you to speed up the learning process. We'll look at many more as we go through the next few chapters.

▶ **Organizing tools.** There's such a wealth of apps, stationery, planners and things available to make life easier. We'll focus on some of the best, as well as how to make the right choices about what to actually use.

▶ **Learning Resources.** Aside from the kind of tools that you can find in shops or online, it's worth also remembering that your tutors often provide hints about tools and resources you should be using. Remember that although when they're marking or analysing your work their job is to look for the 'holes' or imperfections to mark you down as well as the good stuff, it's usually in their best interests that you obtain good results in the end. Sometimes their job even depends on it! So we'll look at learning resources like reading lists and how to use what's in front of you as effectively as possible.

You'll notice that a Study Ninja doesn't just *use* weapons – we've called this characteristic Weapon-*savvy*. The 'savvy' part is very important. Tools are only as useful as the use you make of them. Using all the latest apps or gadgets really badly isn't Weapon-savvy at all, it's a waste of time. So a Ninja knows there's only value in using tools if you're going to use them to save time, make the learning stick and generally get more out of the tool than the effort you put into using it. There's also a temptation to use tools as a distraction technique – after all, who needs to be revising if you're spending all day developing the most elaborate and beautiful revision time-table the world has ever seen? Or who needs to tick things off their to-do list if you can spend all day moving all the items on the list from one prehistoric app that's all of six months old, to the newest, latest, shiniest, all-singing all-dancing new app. We're like magpies, tempted by the shiny and new, especially if it means we don't have to do the difficult stuff for a little while longer. It's important to recognize this tendency. Spending months learning to touch-type on a new keyboard in order to save twenty minutes typing one essay? Not so good. But spending six hours doing a touch-typing class that saves you 40 hours' essay-writing time over the next two years of study? Now that's Weapon-savvy.

STEALTH & CAMOUFLAGE

5. STEALTH AND CAMOUFLAGE

As a Study Ninja, you need to practise the art of Stealth and Camouflage. Getting out of the limelight, getting your head down and finding your focus mojo are important skills. I am writing these words from a beach hut in Sri Lanka. Why? Because I needed several weeks of meticulous Zen-like Calm and Ninja Focus. For that, I needed solitude: away from colleagues who were demanding I stop writing to attend tedious meetings, and away from the temptations and distractions of friends, family, TV, socializing and the day-to-day routines. (And I'll be honest, it's quite good to exchange a few weeks of the English winter for warm sunshine and the sea. Don't hate me.)

GOING DARK

OK, so you might not be able to escape to Sri Lanka every time you have to write an essay, but don't be afraid to spend time 'off the grid'. Doing this deliberately will mark you out as someone with drive and focus. 'Going dark' and making yourself deliberately less available is a tactic adopted by successful business people all the time – they work from home, or they take their teams on 'away days' so that they can think outside of the confines and distractions of the office environment. Likewise, if your usual place to study feels distracting or you need a change of scene, why not leave your phone at home, retreat to a coffee shop nearby, and do a bit of 'tactical hiding'.

CHOOSE YOUR MOMENTS TO STAND OUT

Being too visible at the moment work gets delegated, for instance, is a bad move. It is possible to reduce the proportion of the task done by you and increase what's done by others, just by recognizing where you are in the cycle of things and predicting when the call for action comes. If your friends are discussing the fact that you want to arrange a big weekend away together, there's always one person who gets put in charge of looking into dates or taking on co-ordinating responsibility. I'm not saying your aim should be to avoid all of it but be careful about becoming the go-to person for these kinds of things. Washing up and other household chores are also good examples: again, your aim shouldn't be complete avoidance, but a bit of stealth-mode in relation to these things when you're on a deadline is no bad thing. And sometimes it's good to get a task out of the way. For instance, in a new class, when there was an assignment that I knew would get around to everyone eventually, I'd often make the bold move of going first or close to first, so that I could get mine out of the way. Far better to have the extra thing to do early in the term when there are fewer other commitments, than when the proverbial may be hitting the fan in a few weeks. On a slightly separate note, this is also a great strategy for class discussions or group meetings: say something really insightful early on in the class, get noticed, and then the pressure's off you for the entire rest of the session.

PLAYFUL CAMOUFLAGE

In a world where everyone is increasingly expected to be visible and in the loop at all times, the occasional piece of playful camouflage can be deliciously amusing. I have a friend who, from the age of fifteen right up to the present day, would never say goodbye at the end of the evening. He would quietly slip out, unnoticed, and it often seemed like he vanished into thin air. We might have been at a house party, or in the pub, or at a music gig, or on a day out and we'd suddenly turn around and look at each other and go: 'Where's Jim? Has he gone again?!'

Similarly, in a business context, I have clients who I've coached whose time is eaten up by back-to-back meetings booked into their electronic calendars by their colleagues, leaving them no time to get any of their actual work done, and I've had them come up with deliberately obtuse calendar entries called things like 'project magenta'. If their colleagues see 'project magenta', they don't know what it is (because we made it up), but of course they fear looking foolish so they leave that time alone in the diary. It's sneaky and even a little devious, but it buys back crucial time and focus. Spending time out of the limelight is crucial and our brain and frazzled attention need all the help they can get.

MINDFULNESS

6. MINDFULNESS

When you're in the early years of school, your teachers are there to direct your learning: they tell you what to read, they tell you what to write about and, if one was being cynical, I'd say they tell you how to think. You have very little freedom to learn and express yourself in the way that you want to. But as you progress through your education, and certainly if you are returning to education on your own terms, then I have some great news: you are your own boss! Hooray, you can indulge in self-directed study, follow your own paths, make your own decisions and manage your own learning. Well, it's great news, were it not for the fact that it's also terrifying. The curse of being your own boss is that you have to manage yourself, warts and all.

We will look later in the book at procrastination, fear, laziness, chaotic-thinking and a whole raft of things that become issues once we're managing ourselves.

DON'T JUST DO SOMETHING, SIT THERE

Mindfulness is the technique of noticing the present moment, and in itself is particularly helpful in quietening the chaos of the mind and helping to engender the Zen-like Calm we talked about earlier. Mindfulness meditation is no longer the preserve of hippies, radicals and Buddhists. Its techniques are easily accessible through smart-phone apps and on YouTube.

A MINDFUL APPROACH TO THE MINDLESSNESS OF WORK

For me, mindfulness is a skill to be practised and improved upon. The more I develop and continue the habit of meditating, even for just ten minutes a day, the more I begin to notice other patterns in other moments throughout the day. I come to notice my own bad habits, or when my emotions get in the way of what I'm trying to do, or when my mind is in a loop of craving new data: a kind of hyped up curiosity, hallucinating from one weird YouTube video to another. You might have moments when you notice you're wired and twisted, too?

THE INTENTION OF YOUR ATTENTION

Learning to be present, to make conscious decisions about where we put our attention, is something that mindfulness can really help us achieve. How do you know when this is starting to take effect? You'll notice your own procrastination quicker than before, you'll notice when your attention is 'zoning out' and you're daydreaming rather than constructively reading and you'll notice when you're reacting from a place of high emotion rather than high logic. To be truly mindful is to notice as much about the process of your work and the process of decisions as the time spent thinking about that work and those decisions. In doing so, we listen to ourselves, and pay attention to others, too.

MINDFUL OF OTHERS

I've already hinted that you and I both have our flaws and foibles. We have bad habits, we get things wrong from time to time and we let situations get the better of us sometimes. That's our little secret and I won't tell anyone if you won't. But here's the bigger secret: we're not alone! Everyone else has their struggles and stories, too. Their reactions to your requests when you work together, or to your ruthless but tactful request for a bit of time and space to focus might be because they've taken things the wrong way. Others may criticize you not from a logical place, but from an irrational one. So before we're quick to judge, we should use mindfulness to show a bit of compassion and 'emotional intelligence' in the way we work with others. A little bit of generosity goes a long way – and of course you might need them to return the favour and be as equally understanding of your own needs from time to time!

PREPAREDNESS

7. PREPAREDNESS

There's no point hoping that a few bags of crisps and the occasional energy drink will keep your brain at its optimum level of mental performance. Neither will regular sleep deprivation do you much good. And yet, for many people studying or working, it can be easy to feel guilty if you're taking too much time off to rest and recuperate. When I'm coaching business leaders, I tell them to take full, old-fashioned weekends. This means *two full days* away from the grindstone, off email and preferably doing something completely different. The world has become so pressured that I often sound like a ridiculous idealist for even suggesting people take the breaks from work that they are legally and contractually entitled to (and equally, I know this issue well from my own days as a chaotic and non-Ninja Chief Executive a few years ago, nipping to the office on the weekend to clear my head and clear the inbox).

So instead of feeling guilty about time away from the books or the computer, think about it instead as you 'practising Ninja Preparedness'. Without the breaks, without the mental refresher, we are all at the risk of eventual burnout. Sleep and exercise sit alongside rest and recuperation here as important considerations.

TURNING OVER A NEW LEAF

Bad organizational skills are also an underlying cause of stress and a reason for sub-optimal performance. Is your desk or workspace overflowing with piles of papers, notes and files? Do you know what relates to what? Is it chaos that you know deep down you need to get to grips with, or do you feel like you've got it all under control?

The same can be said for your timetable and basic diary skills. Many people make the mistake of not keeping one coherent diary for the different areas of their life: their study timetable is in one place, but family or work schedules might be kept somewhere else, while social engagements might not even be written down! Again, haphazard and under-prepared systems lead to over-thinking and over-stressing, often pulling away some of your most precious attention.

BEING PREPARED FOR WHEN THE SHIT HITS THE FAN

Now before you finish rolling your eyes at either how basic, or how tedious, this seems, let me spell out the best possible reason for staying prepared.

A Ninja constantly in battle will eventually be killed. There are times in life where we experience 'unexpected turbulence'. Maybe a relationship issue knocks us off course, maybe we spend a few days struck down with an illness, maybe an unexpected work crisis pulls our attention away from what's on our to-do list for a couple of days. In any of these events, what's important is that we're in absolutely the best frame of mind to respond to the danger, and the best possible shape to get things back to normal as quickly as possible.

If you're tired, you're less useful in a crisis. If you're badly organized, you're less agile because you don't have the information you need at your fingertips to be able to re-evaluate all the various things that you're committed to doing, so that you can put them in a new order and carry on. So the speed and quality of your reactions – arguably one of a Ninja's most important traits! – is severely hampered by you being under-prepared.

So this isn't teacher's pet, prefect-and-perfect kind of stuff here. This is just you *assuming* that there'll be trouble ahead, because that's life. And while you can't plan for every eventuality, it's a good idea to plan for the fact that annoying stuff will be along soon to get in your way. When you think about it like that, being prepared doesn't seem so frivolous or annoying at all, does it?

FOCUS

8. FOCUS

How often have you thought to yourself, 'if only I could just focus'? The mind is willing, but the mind is also weak. Well, in the next chapter we'll discuss some of the tricks of self-control that will have you focussing like a Ninja. Of course, prolonged periods of focus can often be difficult, and one of the tricks of Ninja Focus is that short and frequent bursts of focus are better than long sessions burning the midnight oil. It's also important to think about the style of your focus.

THE MULTI-TASKING MYTH

The old time management books preached the virtues of 'multi-tasking'; the idea being that if you can handle a lot of data at one time, make multiple decisions and handle loads of things at any one time, then it'll stand you in good stead to keep on top of your work and get more done. Ironically, the lived experience of the generation currently in school and university, and that of 'Generation Y' (those born and raised in the Eighties and Nineties) is that multi-tasking is part of life. People don't watch TV anymore, they watch a laptop or tablet while they talk to someone else, while also typing messages to someone else, while also standing by for their next social media mention. Communication is set up as a multi-multi-tasking world. Yet while this might be convenient for communication, it's bad for attention and focus.

That holy grail of work-based 'multi-tasking' actually just means regular and rapid re-focussing from one subject or idea or device to another. It's fundamentally fragmented, demented and tiring. So here's how to apply Ninja-like focus. (Perhaps you can guess what I'm about to say – or perhaps not, if at the same time as reading this sentence you're fiddling with your phone. Stop that now!)

Ninjas focus by practising *monotasking*. Staying focussed means staying focussed on ONE THING, until that thing has reached a conclusion. This single thing, when I coach business leaders, is one of the biggest light bulb moments for a lot of people. And while it sounds so simple, it's harder to do than we think. It's also incredibly powerful from a 'user experience' perspective.

How did JK Rowling achieve her success? She sat in a coffee shop, thinking only of one imaginary world, for hours and days and weeks at a time. She monotasked. The same will be said for almost everyone whose work you admire or respect. Be thankful that JK Rowling was not sat in that coffee shop sending Whatsapp messages or checking her Facebook status every five minutes, while also trying to do some freelance graphic design work and learn French from a YouTube channel, because she probably wouldn't have finished the first book yet.

Monotasking also promotes and supports the idea of Zen-like Calm that we mentioned at the beginning of this chapter. It may seem alien and strange, the notion of 'one thing at a time'. You can embrace monotasking simply as a way to produce focus, or you can go further and make it a way of life. It's all about appreciation, focus and a sense of quality not quantity. Here are a few unexpected ways to monotask:

▶ Sitting and doing nothing except being with your thoughts.

▶ Keeping only one thing on your desk (for instance, only the book or folder that relates to the exact thing you're working on).

▶ Leaving your phone off or even at home when having a meal with a loved one.

▶ Leaving the house without your phone at least once a week.

▶ Leaving the room without your phone regularly. (I see you, carrying it around the house!)

FOCUSSING ON YOUR FOCUS

We all live in an age of competing priorities. Focus is something that needs to be thought about and planned. And focus will almost always involve sacrifice too. It will involve a thousand tiny funerals as you mourn the things you actively decide not to do, to leave until tomorrow, or abandon. Friends will miss you, TV will remain unwatched (that's what catchup and streaming were invented for, though) and lots of your little dreams will die. Most of us try to use willpower to win the tug of war between the fun thing we want to do and the thing we know we ought to be doing instead, except we can't bear the sadness of what we're missing, so we lose the battle and give in. We'll look in the next chapter at why self-control is severely overrated. So mourn often and quickly. Get used to mourning the things you won't be doing as part of the process of Focus. Seeing it as a routine part of the process, rather than a constant loss, at least gives you a fighting chance of choosing Focus.

CHEATING TO FOCUS

And yet, relying only on self-control is naive. Choosing other motivators to 'cheat' your way to choosing Focus can be a great way to clear the space. Compete with your friends (she's done HOW many words already?!), ask a family member to monitor your progress so you're motivated not to look foolish or let them down, decide to do just the first five minutes … these are all ways that you can start to develop Focus without even realizing it. We'll talk later in the book about momentum, overcoming procrastination and a whole heap of Ninja tricks and cheats.

CHAPTER 1

HUMAN, NOT SUPERHERO

9. HUMAN, NOT SUPERHERO

By the end of reading this book, you'll know exactly what you need to do to become a Study Ninja. You'll know how to learn and live with increased success. You'll probably even feel a bit smug about it. Your friends may even ask you fawning questions like: 'How do you fit it all in?', 'How did you manage such great results?' and, 'How are you so brilliant at everything?' Because here's the secret: as humans, our default settings for productivity are less than brilliant, and they leave us beating ourselves up so much about our failures that we don't have the time to do things brilliantly. And the biggest travesty of all? So many people accept these default ways of living and working as the only way to do it. What you'll realize is that after the initial effort it takes to change your habits, it's actually *easier* to live as a Study Ninja, with the clarity and ease and effectiveness that it brings, than it is to live without any Ninja skills, fumbling around in the dark. So be prepared to appear like some kind of superhero.

What's also important to remember, though, is that these newly acquired skills don't make you immune from failure. Did Superman ever die or get so tired that he needed a day in bed in any of those films? Do the Power Rangers ever run out of batteries? No, of course not. And most of the books you'll read about study skills, or productivity, or personal development, are written by 'gurus' who seem to have the route to perfection totally mapped out. They're written in a way that asks you to be perfect too, just like they say they are.

So let me make one thing clear. There is no dream of perfection to indulge in here. I don't start this book from the premise that the only thing in your life to think about is your learning. I know you have a life, too. And I don't expect you to be on top of your game the whole time, either. I screw up this stuff regularly. So does everybody else I know, including those that claim they're perfect and immune to failure.

In fact, when I or others in my team screw up, I celebrate it. I celebrate it because it's a gift. The gift is the reminder that we're all beautifully human, full of foibles, carrying around our inner narratives of fear and self-criticism. And that's OK. Think about someone you admire. Maybe a musician or a leader or a businessperson or a TV star. Anyone. Now imagine them five minutes before they're doing what they're famous for. Do you think they're not having the same self doubt that we all have? Do you think they're not cowering at the side of the stage or while they wait for the cameras to roll? Yet to you they seem almost like a superhero.

'Your most unhappy customers are your greatest source of learning'
—Bill Gates

I've built a million-dollar company from scratch in less than a decade, started charities, written books, travelled the world … all things that people praise me for. But there's no perfection here. Even though productivity is my specialist subject, I'm regularly guilty of wildly underestimating how long things will take. I procrastinate with the best of them. I impulsively abandon my plans and do things that have less impact because they're more satisfying to me. I struggle to say no to things. I've improved, with all of these things. But the biggest improvement of all was realizing that it's ok to fail or get things wrong every now and again. In fact, realizing your human limitations while developing a passing resemblance to a superhero is a powerful combination.

And that's what will happen as you embrace the way of the Study Ninja. We're on this journey together, not to make everything perfect in your world, but to get you to a place where you can achieve everything you want with only a requisite number of hiccups along the way. Others may look at you differently, wondering if you're some kind of superhero, but you'll know the truth.

A Ninja has great tools and skills. Despite having lots on their plates, they don't feel overwhelmed; and despite the occasional hiccup, they're calm and in control. They're Prepared, Focussed and they're occasionally Ruthless. But a Ninja is always human. No special powers or perfection here. Just a human being, doing their best – and humans achieving greatness, against all the odds, is way more interesting and impressive than the coolest superhero.

2. GETTING ORGANIZED

SCAFFOLDING, SECOND BRAINS AND REGULAR NINJA RITUALS

Live as if you were to die tomorrow.
Learn as if you were to live forever.'
—Mahatma Gandhi

WHY GET ORGANIZED?

I saw you rolling your eyes. 'Get organized? Do I have to?' It's a question and an attitude that I myself had for many years. In fact, I'm not an organized person at all. My general working style is the opposite: conceptual, impulsive, chaotic, instinctive, creative. I'm a classic 'don't box me in' kind of guy. But after years of realizing my completely inadequate personal organizational skills were failing me badly (and hampering my considerable ambitions), I decided to do something about it. So what this means for you is two very important things: firstly, if one of the most naturally disorganized people on the planet can learn this stuff, so can you; and secondly, at every level in this chapter, I feel your pain. Of course, you may be really organized already, in which case my experience is you're even more likely to make changes as a result of this chapter, because you see the value of being organized and efficient already, but my experience is that whatever your starting point, adopting the habits in this chapter can be life-changing. And believe me, I don't use the word 'life-changing' lightly. This chapter may actually change your life. Your friends and family will look at you differently, you'll look at yourself differently, you'll feel better, and your life will be easier.

In this chapter I'm going to talk about the scaffolding you need to juggle learning and life. That is, the frameworks and structures that hold everything together. We'll start with looking at where to keep everything in your life, then we'll look at Checklists to help make some great habits stick and finally we'll cover some Ninja rituals: little ways to approach every day, week and term to ensure not just effective study but a happier life.

PAY ATTENTION

It's often said that time is your most precious resource. Time is certainly a great leveller – no-one, however rich, can buy more time – but there is one resource even more precious: your attention. It's important to see the job of 'being organized' as something that will help you manage your attention most efficiently, rather than helping you 'manage time'.

The reason attention is a more precious resource than time is that our attention can get split and fragmented a hundred different ways. If you're trying to concentrate on five things at once, you're actually not concentrating on any of them very well, and your fragmented attention becomes less than the sum of its parts. Likewise, even when we learn to focus in on one thing at a time, we have periods in the day where physiologically, we're just not on form. You might be a morning person or a night owl, for instance, and when you start to really analyse it, you might notice certain hours in the day where you generally feel more awake and hours where you just feel more sluggish. How you work should fit in with these different levels of attention, in order to make the most of it.

YOUR THREE LEVELS OF ATTENTION:

1. **Proactive Attention.** This is where you are fully focussed, alert, in the zone and ready to tackle the hardest piece of coursework or get your head around the most difficult concept. How you use this level of attention and what you do with it plays a big role in your success or failure.

2. **Active Attention.** OK, you're not quite at the very top of your game, but you're moving along nicely. You might be quite easily distracted. You might, in this mode, be occasionally brilliant but also find yourself doing some more sloppy work. While Active isn't as valuable as its Proactive counterpart, it's still a useful and important resource.

3. **Inactive Attention.** We all have those periods where we're just not up to much. In fact, one modern disease is 'flogging a dead horse' – convincing yourself that you still have another hour left in you before bed, even though you can't get out of the loop of YouTube videos or stalking celebrities on Twitter. We convince ourselves that Inactive attention can be useful. The truth is, it can be, but only if we're organized enough to have saved up things to do that specifically don't require much attention.

So how much of each of these three types of attention do you think you have in a typical day? And what do you currently spend that attention on? Let's look at a typical day in your life (I appreciate some of the hours below will involve a fourth level of attention called 'No Attention Possible', which is better known by its acronym, NAP …).

EXERCISE: MY ATTENTION LEVELS

Look at the table overleaf and think about an average day in your life. Where are the peaks and troughs of attention? Put a tick in each time period, choosing either Proactive Attention, Active Attention or Inactive Attention.

Before you fill this in, promise me honesty. Bear in mind that in an average day, I probably have 2–3 hours of Proactive Attention. That's it. Then a few hours of Active Attention and a couple of hours of Inactive attention. If you're a morning person, yours might start strong and then fade through the day, but think about post-meal lulls, second winds, how you use caffeine or other stimulants and what else is going on around you on a typical day. Of course, this is just your 'best guess' and isn't scientific, but it will hopefully give you a flavour of what you might be able to do to help manage your attention later in this chapter.

Time	Proactive	Active	Inactive
Before 6am			
6am			
7am			
8am			
9am			
10am			
11am			
12pm			
1pm			
2pm			
3pm			
4pm			
5pm			
6pm			
7pm			
8pm			
9pm			
10pm			
11pm			
Midnight and later			

So that's a typical day, if such a thing exists! But perhaps your weekly schedule is a little different. You can create your own weekly timetable document or download a PDF worksheet to map this out at: www.studyninja.online/resources

Maybe Monday mornings after that statistics lecture just feel a bit 'ugh', or Wednesday nights out mean Thursday mornings are a write-off? Perhaps you have the house to yourself all morning on Fridays? Perhaps those quiet times on the train make great reading times?

DISTRACTION VS ATTENTION

Let's talk more about distractions. In particular, three huge reasons that account for about 95% of your distractions:

1. Procrastination
2. Shiny new things
3. Nags

Let's look at each of these three things in turn.

PROCRASTINATION

We procrastinate for many reasons, but typically there are four main ones that turn your mind, your attention and your ambitions to DUST: Difficult work, Undefined Work, a Scary outcome at the end of the work and work that's just, well, Tedious.

Difficult !! # *

Undefined ?

Scary

Tedious Zzz

We will focus lots of practical attention on the issue of procrastination in its own chapter, so skip straight to Chapter 9 if right now what you really want is a multitude of ways to get going or keep going, but for now let's talk more about where your procrastination actually comes from.

Our fears and survival instincts come from a part of the brain, the limbic system, that shouts louder and processes information more quickly than the frontal cortex (the more rational, smarter and logical part of the brain). So the battle going on inside your head is destined to be one that the rational and motivated part of you struggles to win. So we lead ourselves into temptation. We seek distractions, we tie ourselves in knots with worry or we just 'zone out' and do nothing at all. All of this is perfectly natural and human. You'll never stop procrastinating entirely. However, you can learn to spot the patterns of behaviour that lead to procrastination and get back on track more quickly.

There's no voodoo magic to it – great systems promote great thinking and help you reduce distractions. Speaking of which …

SHINY NEW THINGS

The next type of distraction comes in the form of the shiny new thing. Shiny new things are great new ideas, exciting smartphone alerts, new emails, something interesting happening outside of the window, something 'live' on the radio, TV or internet that if you miss now you'll never see again: basically anything exciting or new. We like shiny new things. We especially like them if they take us away from dull but important things. Someone asked me recently when it is that I come up with the best ideas for a book. I realized that the answer is 'usually when I'm in the middle of writing the previous book'. And that's because books are hard work, but shiny new ideas that I don't actually have a *commitment* to right now are just a playground for the mind. It's a place you can explore, with no consequences, like a daydream that's somehow permitted because it feels useful. Likewise, whatever's shouting latest and loudest from an email inbox or a phone home screen often feels like the most important piece of information in the world, because it's something new for our mind to focus on.

NAGS

'Nags' is a technical term I came up with a few years ago. It describes those thoughts – and occasionally those people! – that remind you of something important that you need to do. It would be wonderful if such a reminder came at a moment you weren't engaged in other useful work, but alas, we can't control when any particular nag occurs. For example, it would be wonderful if my brain reminded me that we've run out of milk at home just as I drive past the last shop I'll see before I get back. But somehow my brain forgets to do this until I get home, pour some cereal into a bowl, open the door of the fridge looking for milk and … oh.

The same is true for the kind of nags that occur in our work and study. As you're sitting there reading, or writing an essay, your brain says, 'when is the exam again? The 25th or the 28th? How many more days do I have to revise after I've finished this essay?' And as soon as that nag is there, it's the loudest little thought in your mind. You can't get rid of the nasty little thing. So you scrabble around looking for that printout of the exam schedule, you go online, you message a friend. And all the while, your essay isn't getting finished.

This leads us nicely to how a Ninja deals with all three of these kinds of distractions, either to minimize them or manage them. A Ninja uses a Second Brain.

A NINJA'S SECOND BRAIN

At times, your brain can be an utterly sophisticated tool. At other times, your brain can be an utter tool. Think about it. The human mind has fuelled incredible human progress: put people on the moon, solved the most incredible mathematic equations, produced beautiful pieces of art. And yet I'm sure you've come across the game, 'I went to the shops and I bought ...' In that game, your job is to say a thing, then the next person says your thing and adds a thing, and as you go around the circle, the idea is that you try to remember everything in the right order. It's hard! If you get past about a dozen things in that game, you're doing well. We'll talk more about memory techniques later, which can aid your performance in games like that, but the point here is that short-term memory is much less sophisticated than other, more logical and creative parts of the brain.

Have you ever felt a bit overwhelmed with new ideas (shiny new things) or with nags, and then sat down to write a list of them all? Did you feel better afterwards? When you did that, you didn't finish all of those things, or even deal with the thorny questions of which were more important, but what you did was relieve your short-term memory of the job of trying to hold on to all of those things. By doing this, you develop a sense of control, because that little piece of paper can actually start to do the remembering for you. And it works. Sort of.

Lots of to-do lists feel great when you first use them, and then over time you lose the trust that that list really does hold the key to everything you need to do, and as more things clutter up your short-term memory and you forget to add them to the list, you begin to distrust the list. If you've ever found yourself rewriting a to-do list or transferring it from one place to another, you'll understand now why you did that!

So as a Study Ninja you need a list that you know you can trust. Something a little more sophisticated than the back of an envelope or a Post-it note. What you really need is a complete list of all the projects you're working on and all the tasks that relate to those projects. And that, my friend, is a Second Brain.

WHAT DOES A SECOND BRAIN LOOK LIKE?

A Second Brain can take any form you like, but here are some of the most common:

▶ An app that works on your smartphone, tablet and on the web. I use a fancy one called Nozbe, which also allows me to collaborate with my assistant, but there are lots of others in different price ranges and most can be bought very cheaply. Have a look at Toodledo and Todooist for two very good examples. The beauty of these apps is that they sync between your devices, and they're also accessible as web-based apps so you can use them on library computers or work computers, without the need to download software.

▶ a Google doc or Microsoft Word doc

▶ your normal full-sized notebook (tip: use the back for projects and actions, leaving the front free for notes)

▶ if you use Microsoft Office as part of your job, the Tasks section in Outlook (using category view to make it a bit more user-friendly).

Basically, anything that can hold a few lists and that you're comfortable using makes a fine Second Brain.

WHAT GOES IN YOUR SECOND BRAIN?

There are two main lists that you need to create in your Second Brain, the Projects List and the Master Actions List. The Projects List gives you the 'helicopter overview' whereas the Master Actions List gives you the view from the ground; the practical things you need to do, like speak to people or send emails or write down ideas.

PROJECTS LIST

I would define a project as 'a collection of actions, leading to a desired outcome'. You might be working on a dozen or more projects at any one time. The idea behind having a Projects List is that it gives you an overview of your whole life, helping answer the question: 'What am I committed to at the moment?' In the interests of Balance, it's best that you think about stuff as projects that you previously may not have thought were projects at all. For example, if you're going on a safari holiday to Kenya, you might have a project which is 'prepare for Kenya trip', which would include all the things from making sure you have your camera ready to getting to the doctors to have your tropical disease immunizations. Likewise, attending that cookery course, playing in a band or getting in control of student finances are all things I would suggest fall into the category of 'projects'. Why? Because you want your Second Brain to remember all these things, and you want to have the ability to see everything you're spending time on, all in one place, so that you can start to make better decisions about where you're spending your precious attention and time.

EXERCISE: PROJECTS

What projects do you have in your life right now? Here are a few triggers, to get you thinking about the kinds of areas of your life where you might have projects.

Remember, Projects are NOT tasks or actions. They are collections of tasks or actions. For example, one of my 'home projects' here is 'Move House'. Within this project, I will need to sign the contracts for the new place, arrange a moving date, research and arrange transport to help me move (or call Mum and Dad!), pack up my stuff, sort out keys, arrange meter readings for gas and electricity and so on. But I don't want this stuff on my Projects List. We'll get on to where we put the actions in a moment, but for now, just think BIG and focus only on the projects themselves.

Home projects

E.g. 'Move house'

_____

_____

_____

Personal projects

E.g. 'Organize Gran's birthday celebration'

_____

_____

_____

Academic work projects

E.g. 'Complete and hand in the semiotics essay before Monday 21st'

_____

_____

_____

Paid work projects

E.g. 'Finish the inventory of products by Friday 18th'

_____

_____

_____

Voluntary work

E.g. 'Create the new website I promised my friend's charity in time for their fundraiser in November'

_____

_____

_____

Blank category* _____

_____

_____

_____

Blank category* _____

_____

_____

_____

*add your own categories here – there are no right or wrong answers, just whatever helps you see and manage the different areas of your life!

_____

So now you have the overview of your entire life, via the Projects List. This is something so few people ever sit down and do properly. I've worked with some of the most senior business people in the world, and many of them have no such list at all, while others have work plans and strategies here, personal bits of paper there, a few things written on their computer desktop in little notes or in a paper diary, but very rarely will they have everything outlined on a Projects List. And yet once they do this and keep it updated, they find it a hugely valuable tool, because it gives enormous clarity to see everything side by side, everything in balance. It also offers perspective: if you're using a Projects List regularly and keeping it updated, you have more power to say 'no' to new things, precisely because you see so much more clearly when you're overloaded.

And of course, you also have the power to change your mind about what projects are on the list. The list you just wrote is a list of the things you're committed to right now, today. Tomorrow, you may decide you need to renegotiate it. You might decide you don't need to have such a big party and you'd rather have a small gathering that's easier and quicker to arrange, or that you don't have the time for that voluntary project that you promised. The sooner you realize this and confront it, the happier you'll be. Admittedly renegotiating projects with others is more difficult than renegotiating the ones with just yourself involved, but in the long run people prefer you to be hon-est if you can't commit to something rather than for you to struggle along getting nowhere, only to let them down later on when they don't have time to involve anyone else. A bit of Ninja Ruthlessness here goes a long way, and it's much easier to be Ruthless when you can see the whole picture – saying no to something is often the best way of saying yes to something else that might be more valuable.

THE LANGUAGE WE USE WITH OURSELVES

To get to that place of Zen-like Calm that a Ninja strives for, it's very important that we're really clear about the things we actually have to do. So before we discuss the Master Actions List, let me give you a five-minute crash course in how to write great actions; the kind that are so common-sense, yet rarely commonplace, on the average to-do list.

There's one question that if you ask it to yourself regularly, and ask it about each and every project or new idea, will reduce 95% of your stress. It's simple, yet subtly powerful. That question is:

'WHAT'S THE NEXT PHYSICAL ACTION?'

Most project planners will tell you to write long lists of every step of the project, and sometimes it's certainly useful to have a good idea of the 'milestones' – in other words, the 'stages' of a project. But doing this can often lead to getting stuck. When you don't know *exactly* how to get started, you don't know how to create the momentum to succeed. So let's break down this key question word by word:

NEXT. There may be more than one thing you can do next, but next means you can take the action without waiting for anything else to happen first. For example, if the project is 'complete and hand in my English Literature essay about Hamlet', you might have a number of things you can do next: sketching out structure ideas in your note-book, reading a commentary book that talks about Shakespeare's intentions for Hamlet's character, reading the actual text itself, watching a film version, writing up your lecture notes, calling your friend to talk about their views on Hamlet. So you could do any of these things next. They're all 'next' physical actions. But printing or submitting the essay, even though it will need to be done, is not a next physical action, because you have to do the research and writing stages first. It'll be an action one day, but not right now. So for now, you don't need to make a note of printing. Put your Ninja Focus only on what's next.

PHYSICAL. To be really clear on the action, you should be able to picture how it will be done. Will you be sat at a desk? Will you be in the library? Typing? Scribbling? Reading? Talking to someone on the phone or face to face? The use of the word 'physical' here helps you to put it in your mind's eye. And that visualization, if you start to think in this way, actually becomes the start of the process of doing it, because the momentum is now created.

ACTION. An action should involve a verb. When you first think of something, and it pops into your head as a nag or a shiny new thing, it's rarely action-focussed. Usually the focus on that thought is the observation that we have a commitment to something or there's somebody that we're worried about letting down. Or we're aware of some new opportunity that needs our attention, and that we'd better start thinking about that thing. So if we 'capture' these thoughts by writing them down we tend to capture a noun: 'Dave!' 'Essay deadline?!' 'Train tickets!' 'Mum!' 'Birthday!'

For these to be next physical actions, and to actually feel doable, we need to add verbs to the nouns. This sounds small and pedantic, I know, but here's the point: if you look at a to-do list with a whole load of nouns on it, your brain has so much work to do before you're at the stage where you even know what your *choices* are, let alone before you can get to the stage of knowing the best use of your attention right now, or the most important thing from the list to tackle. So if you've ever been sat with your to-do list, but still felt stuck, this is what's happening. Think about it: having a to-do list and still feeling stuck is absolutely absurd. And it's this broken, bad-habit-driven style of to-do lists that cripples people with procrastination.

Making it immediate, physical and action-focussed, and imagining the action in your mind is a very powerful Ninja tip. But it takes practice. Here are some example Next Physical Actions and some of their less-than-ideal counterparts. Which kind do you normally see on your own to-do list?

Bad examples of to-do list items	Good examples of 'next physical actions'
Granny	Call mum re: ideas granny's birthday present & time of meal
Do Essay	Sketch out chapter headings for Hamlet essay on paper
Parking	Go online and renew parking permit before 20th (deadline)
Finish Essay	Print out & read current draft of essay, make notes
mobile	Get back to 3 mobile about upgrade 0845 606060
Becky's birthday	Ask Becky on Facebook messenger about dress code for party

To get from the bad examples to the good ones requires a little bit of extra thinking – a bit more Ninja Focus – but doing so makes your list so much easier to read, and importantly, so much easier to actually *do* something with! So now we're going to look at the structure of this most vital of lists, the Master Actions List.

MASTER ACTIONS LIST

The Master Actions List is where you keep all of those Next Physical Actions we've just been talking about. And whereas you only really need to keep track of the Projects List once a week or even once a fortnight, the Master Actions List should be part of your daily routine. Think of the Master Actions List as part of your dashboard or control centre. It's where you make the choices about what's best to do and when, because it contains the complete 'memory' of *all* the possible things that you could do next when you have time and attention available.

LET'S TALK SPACE AND TIME

The Master Actions List is most useful when you can instantly see what's possible, given your current time, space or place. In the library? Well, Master Actions List, show me the things I said I needed the library to do. Online? Show me the research, the online banking, the emails I need to send and other online tasks. Sat on a plane or on the underground? Give me a list of the things that don't need any connection to the outside world at all – the thinking, reading, idea-generation, problem-solving … The Master Actions List is also great for storing up a list of things you need to tell or ask your boss or your personal tutor. And it's also great if you've got particular kinds of work that you can 'batch' together – for example, half the effort of online shopping is getting on there, remembering your password, inputting payment details and so on. So while you're already logged in, it makes sense to get as many of the things you need ordered as you can in one go. Batching up actions can really save time and attention. One of my least favourite things in running my business is talking to the government helplines about the tax we need to pay, or regulations we have to follow. This is, admittedly, partly because I hate the idea that I'm now a grown-up who has to deal with such things, but it's also partly because their hold queues, bureaucratic systems and 'computer says no' attitude is enough to put most people off running their own business for life. So I batch these things up and wait until there are five or six things I need, so that by the time I'm wasting my Friday afternoon on hold for half an hour to them, I know it'll be worth it for the ticks on my list when I hang up the phone.

So having your next physical actions grouped together by 'Place' (where you need to be do them) or 'Space' (the 'mode' of work you need to be in) is useful for all sorts of reasons. If you've ever cursed yourself for reading awful, three-year-old magazines in the dentist's waiting room, or mindlessly scrolling on your phone because you feel like there's nothing else to do, then the Master Actions List will give you some choices of other things to do in those specific moments.

WHAT CATEGORIES SHOULD I USE?

There is no set way to categorize your Master Actions List, other than grouping things by places and spaces. There's a good reason why I can't just give you the answer here, and that is because my life is different from yours! However, below are some suggested categories. You might only choose one or two, or you might choose all of these and more, but the important thing is that you can change it and adapt it as you go along: use Ninja Mindfulness to be conscious of which parts of the list you're using well and which parts seem confused in your head. If you're not sure whether something goes on your 'campus' list or your 'in lectures' list, perhaps you should merge them. If you're regularly finding yourself stuck because your 'home' list has coursework but also household chores, perhaps separate it out so that you have a 'home chores' and 'home study' list. It's all about experimentation and it won't be 100% right for you straight away – and your needs will change at different times in your life too.

But having said that, here are a few suggestions that I think, as a student, you should think very seriously about adopting, and then a few more that might be slightly more 'optional' or might not apply to your world.

Strong suggestions:

▶ At my desk/computer

▶ Online (having this as a separate state to 'on my computer' will help with Ninja Stealth and Camouflage, and help you manage the time you spend online)

▶ On campus

▶ Offline

▶ At home

▶ With personal tutor (use this for storing up questions as well as actions)

A few others you might consider:

▶ With parents/family

▶ At my job

▶ Reading

▶ On the train/bus (this one could easily be merged with reading if you have regular long journeys and you can read on the train)

▶ At my desk with Proactive Attention

▶ At my desk with Inactive Attention

▶ At my volunteering project

▶ With my band/choir/book group/etc

EXAMPLE OF A STUDENT'S MASTER ACTIONS LIST

Home chores

▶ Do the washing up

▶ Wash clothes

▶ Tidy bedroom

Home study

▶ File away this week's lecture notes

▶ Go through emails for information from the School Office about guest speaker lectures

▶ Brainstorm ideas for research proposal due on 6th November

Campus

▶ Visit Lynne in her office hour to discuss dissertation ideas

▶ Go to the library and pay late book fine

▶ Hand in essay title request form to Melanie's office

▶ Meet Martin in the library to discuss group presentation

▶ Email Katie about work experience with her mum

▶ Go to the library and find some books for Forensic Linguistics reading

▶ Go to campus shop and buy toothpaste

Computer

▶ Print off all of this week's lecture notes

▶ Research dissertation ideas online

▶ Parents/family

▶ Call Mum about going home for the weekend

▶ Reply to Dad's email about Student Finance

Job

▶ Ring Paul about changing shifts at the weekend

▶ Look at next week's hours on staff rota

Social/friends

▶ Look online for birthday present ideas for Ruby

▶ Transfer Jess £15 petrol money

▶ Ask Taz and Rachel about best date for John's surprise party

WHAT ABOUT SINGLE ACTIONS THAT DON'T HAVE A PROJECT?

While a lot of what you need to do will be connected to a project, there will be those little things that are nothing more than single actions: the paying of a bill, the returning of a library book, the single online purchase or the downloading of a movie or musician's new album. These are just single actions, so you don't need to make them part of a project at all, just add them to the Master Actions List as single actions.

EXERCISE: FROM PROJECTS TO ACTIONS

OK, now it's time for us to stop talking about lists and for you to make your own! This might take twenty minutes, or if you're hyper-busy and have a lot of projects on that Projects List that you made earlier, you might want to clear an hour to do this. But trust me, once you've done it this time, you'll have a pretty up-to-date list every time you come back to look at it again, so you'll never have as much thinking and writing to do on this as you have right now. In other words, the more you do this, the quicker it gets, and the more it starts to develop Ninja-level clarity and productivity.

1. First, grab your Projects List from earlier. Even if you plan to use an app or do the list electronically later, you might want to just do this first bit on paper, so that you can get used to doing the thinking first.

2. Have a read of those categories and make some headings on paper of the ones that you think you'll definitely use for your Master Actions List. Leave some space though, because you'll think of other categories later!

3. Go through each project in turn. Ask yourself the question: 'What's the next physical action?' Write down the action, parking it in its category. Remember, there may be more than one next physical action on certain projects, in which case, write down all of the actions you can think of – but they must be things you can do *next*, not actions for further along in the project!

4. Continue until you've written down at least one next physical action for each project on your Projects List. When you get to the end, have a quick think about other one-off actions: things that you need to do, but that don't have a project. Add these, too.

5. Sit back, make a cup of tea and admire your new, Second Brain. It may not look like much right now, but this thing will become a big part of your life as a Study Ninja, and it will result in Zen-Like Calm and a feeling of profound Preparedness that you never thought possible. Yes, you're finally on top of everything you need to get done, and you've got the tools to stay calm and in control, no matter how big that list is.

THE QUESTION OF TRUST

Now that you've developed a super-duper Projects List and a gleaming new Master Actions List, you might want to play around with one of the apps I mentioned, so that you can start carrying your Second Brain with you wherever you go, because you never know when a new idea might strike, or when you might have a little unexpected pocket of time and attention you can fill.

The next few weeks are particularly important, as you get used to using your new Second Brain. Why? Because a new habit takes some time and practice to become natural, and because there's a profound difference between *nearly* trusting your Second Brain and *completely* trusting it. Knowing that the lists are a genuine reflection of your commitments means your own brain is 'freed' to concentrate on things like learning, creativity and having a life. Once your Second Brain earns your trust, you'll walk around feeling a bit lighter, less weighed down by everything. And the way you learn to trust it? You use it. You look at it. You add to it. You check that there aren't loads of other nags or shiny new things rattling around in your brain – and if there are, write them down and add them to your Master Actions List.

DAILY RITUALS

With a Master Actions List, a Study Ninja is Prepared and ready to face the day. Whether it's a day of lectures and seminars with the odd hour free thrown in for good measure, or a day at work trying to squeeze in an hour of study, a Daily Ritual will help promote a bit of Ninja Mindfulness and keep you on track.

We talked earlier about the importance of managing your attention and focus. Your attention will peak and dip in some regular patterns, but let's be honest, we all have days where we get out of bed feeling like we just don't want to face anything. When that happens, I want to spot it as early as possible and adjust my plans accordingly. This is why a Daily Ritual can be extremely useful to make sure you manage your attention and energy to its optimum. With a little Ninja Mindfulness, you can get in touch with yourself, your emotions, your body and your moods. My Daily Ritual involves just two things. First, I go for a mile run. A mile takes me no more than about ten minutes, so I know it's manageable no matter how busy I'm going to be that day. Next, I sit down with a cup of tea, a pen and a Post-it note and ask myself a few questions, to set myself up for the day. Mine are:

1. How's my energy today? How am I feeling?

2. What's in my calendar? (Really I'm asking myself what's a hard-wired commitment like a meeting or a travel plan, versus what's free time for me to choose how to fill it. And of course, I'm thinking particularly about when that free time comes, and what kind of level of attention I can expect at those times.)

3. If today was a success, what would be achieved? (I keep this realistic; what are the two or three key things that I want to put a real focus and effort on? To figure this out, I look through my Master Actions List and pick out two or three really key actions to focus on. I write these items down onto a Post-it note.)

4. Out of those tasks, what feels Difficult, Undefined, Scary or Tedious? (Remember 'DUST'?)

5. What's my best strategy for how I schedule everything in today?

By the end of this short piece of thinking, which takes no longer than five minutes, a couple of things have happened. Firstly, I've got a Post-it note filled with the main things I need to do. This is basically my Daily To-Do List. Also, I've spent a few minutes just being Mindful about my intentions. Most people start their day by checking Facebook or email – which when you think about it, is starting your day with a focus on everyone else's priorities, not your own! (Note: I'm not holier than thou at all – I will sometimes be prone to surfing the web in bed before I get up, but I've deleted Facebook and email from my phone specifically to get out of these particularly bad habits, as it's the only way I don't give in to the temptation!)

So that's my Daily Ritual, but yours can involve all kinds of things. I used to have a much longer one that involved a bit of meditation, exercises as well as running, an elaborate breakfast routine and so on. But I found that my days often start in a rush, or I'm pressured to get early trains to places, or I'm starting the day in a hotel somewhere I don't know ... there were just too many days that were not a 'typical day' and I felt like the habit of my longer ritual was lapsing. So I focussed it down just to those two important things: a short run and a five-minute piece of Mindfulness to prepare me for the day. Fifteen minutes from warm bed to Post-it note in hand. And because it's so short, it really feels like cheating now if I skip it!

Often I speak to people who don't have a Daily Ritual to start their days, but they wish they did. My answer to this is always: 'How do you expect to change your habits if you don't think about your habits?' And a quick few minutes spent designing a new routine can work wonders. So now I'd like you to design your own Daily Ritual, to be done first thing in the morning, every morning. It can involve whatever you like, and it can be simple or strenuous. I've put a few suggestions below of things you could make part of your Daily Ritual, but it's totally up to you what you pick. The only guidance I'll give from experience is don't overload your Ritual with too many things – keep it simple.

Examples:

▶   a quick morning run

▶   ten press-ups/sit-ups

▶   yoga

▶   meditation

▶   prayer

▶   preparing and eating breakfast

▶   reading the morning newspaper

▶   walking the dog

▶   walking on your own

▶ stretches

▶ feeding your pet

▶ reading a few pages of a book

▶ writing a journal

▶ watering the plants/watering the garden

▶ drinking tea/coffee

▶ thinking about your day

▶ asking yourself questions about your level of energy, motivation, task selections and potential procrastinations

▶ checking your Master Actions List and writing/compiling a Daily To-Do List (hint: whatever else you pick, pick this one!).

DAILY TO-DO LIST

Let's talk a little more about the Daily To-Do List. Before, in your pre-Ninja world, a single to-do list might have been all you had. Yet now we're setting up a list for Projects, another one called a Master Actions List and now another one called the Daily To-Do List. You might be thinking, 'isn't this just list overload?' or, 'do I really need three lists?' But each list has a specific purpose in an approach to work and life that's designed to lower your stress levels. You need a Projects List for the overview, you need a Master Actions List so that your brain doesn't have to remember all the things you actually have to do and so that you have the best possible information available to you each day, and your Daily To-Do List helps you focus on what you actually plan to do that day. You could *never* finish your entire Master Actions List in a day, so there's always a relationship between the Master Actions List and a Daily To-Do List. Think of the Master Actions List as some kind of huge container filled with stuff, and each morning you reach into the container and pick out the best bits of stuff for that day. During the day, you might only look at those things that you picked out and are now sat on your desk or in your bag, or you might go back and forth between the 'container' and your little list, if you reach the end of what's on that little list and want more, or just want to change your mind and mix things up again.

WEEKLY RITUALS

With the Second Brain fully functioning and a Daily Ritual established, you're well on the way to being the most organized person you know, as well as the calmest Ninja around!

The tough part is making the habit stick. I'm sure you've started a new habit or a new way of working many times before and had a burst of enthusiasm for a few weeks, only to see it fall away a few weeks later. And when that happens, you feel even worse than before, because not only are you back to your old habits but you feel like a failure for not making it stick. It's actually worse this way than not having tried to change your habits at all! This is a very common experience, and it's important to recognize why habits like keeping an up-to-date Second Brain or practising a Daily Ritual don't work. My experience is that it's often down to a lack of mindful and conscious thought about:

A.   The habit itself: what *exactly* are you trying to change, and achieve by this change?

B.   The positive resulting behaviour: when it goes well, why is that?

C.   The negative behaviour: when it goes badly or doesn't happen, what is it that's getting in the way?

Spending some time reflecting on these questions is just one of the several benefits of adopting a Weekly, Monthly or Termly Checklist. These checklists are designed to keep you on course, practising the right habits, and most importantly, help the Clever, Motivated version of you to support the Lazy, Scatterbrained version of you to get things back on track when you find your new habits slipping (see page 95).

WHAT IS A CHECKLIST?

The Daily Ritual we discussed earlier is really no more than a very simple version of a checklist. In Atul Gawande's book *The Checklist Manifesto*, he describes how simple checklists, adopted by highly experienced surgeons, reduced human error significantly and saved lives. The checklist included simple steps like 'wash hands' that perhaps we take for granted. But whether it's brain surgery or being a good student, one of the secrets of success is so obvious it's often overlooked: do the simple things consistently and well.

Checklists help us do the simple things and do them well. I have a Weekly Checklist that I go through every Friday (and if I'm too busy during the week, I do it on Saturdays, because I've learned it's that vital to my success). The Checklist helps me review that week's progress, helps me spend a few minutes reviewing and updating the Projects List and Master Actions List so that my Second Brain feels fresh, up to date and fully functioning, and generally just helps me plan ahead so that I'm on top of all the things I have coming up. I am regularly managing 80–100 projects on my Projects List. They don't all require an action every week, but they do require at least a moment's thought on a weekly basis so that I don't overlook things.

The Weekly Checklist keeps me sane. While it's important to spend those few moments thinking about the progress of each project, what's really vital with this habit is that I'm diving deep down into that Second Brain. I'm checking that I still trust it. And trust has to be earned, so I'm also doing the thinking that's required for the Second Brain to remain relevant to me. Once, as part of what I call my 'extreme productivity experiments' I tried to live without any of these things for a month. For a week or so, it was blissful, because I felt like there was much less to do; I didn't need to write things down into my Second Brain lists any more, and I felt much freer with my thinking and decisions. But once I lost the trust that my Second Brain was as reliable as my brain, I had to do all of that thinking again on my own: I had to try to remember – in my own head! – what was happening with all of those projects and what to do next. I found myself scribbling makeshift to-do lists on the backs of envelopes, only to lose them or realize that the really important stuff wasn't written down on them … Suddenly I was *really* stressed. In many ways it was good because it proved that the methods that I teach actually work – and actually are the most efficient way you can work – but those last three weeks of stress are something I never want to experience again.

At the end of a Weekly Checklist, I feel physically different, too. I coast into the weekend feeling lighter, better, more focussed, excited to start the following week. All of this is about clarity. When I teach people to develop their very own Weekly Checklist, you can see the light bulb turn on in their heads – it's as if they've discovered the missing piece to a particularly painful or difficult jigsaw! And it does feel like that when you start to implement it and use it.

I'm going to ask you in a moment to create your own Weekly Checklist. Just like with the Daily Ritual we discussed, where you wrote down things personal to you, there's no right or wrong way to set up a Weekly Checklist, but there *are* some fundamental stages to the process. So let me first outline those, and then much like I did with the Daily Ritual ideas, I'll offer some suggestions for things you might like to do at each stage.

THE FIVE STAGES OF A WEEKLY CHECKLIST:
Stage 1 – What's new?

Stage 2 – Get your Second Brain up to date

Stage 3 – Think ahead

Stage 4 – Practical Preparedness

Stage 5 – Questions

Stage 1 – What's new?

This is where you check a few different places to see if there are new inputs – new things you need to consider and make sure you have covered in your Second Brain. It's really about getting up to date if you've had a busy week, and making sure that you're reacting appropriately to what's emerging. Ideas for this include:

▶ Check through your emails. Any shiny new things or nags?

▶ Check in your brain! Ask yourself what's new, what's bugging you, what needs attention

▶ File, process or review any lectures notes

▶ Check and see if there's anything in your bag (like forms that need filling in or bits of information you need to keep hold of

▶ Check your notebook. Anything new there to capture in your Second Brain or deal with (particularly actions or potential new projects)

▶ Check social media. Anything there you've promised to do? (Make sure you get out of social media as soon as you've checked, or you'll risk falling into the vortex and getting sidetracked!)

Stage 2 – Get your Second Brain up to date

This stage is about re-familiarizing yourself with your Second Brain. It's all about your regular brain interacting with your Second Brain and checking they're both on the same wavelength.

▶ Go through your calendar or diary for two weeks behind and three weeks ahead. What's on the horizon? Add new projects or actions to your Second Brain.

▶ Check the Master Actions List so that you're really clear about what everything there means – look for things that are still on the list that you might have done but not yet crossed off!

▶ Are there new actions you can think of as you look through the Master Actions List?

▶ Are there actions that you can force yourself to delete or delegate to someone else? (I make sure I force-delete three things every week and force-delegate three things every week. This is hard, but it's a great way to build the habit of Ninja Ruthlessness, as even 'good-to-do' things get the chop!)

Stage 3 – Think ahead

The focus in this stage shifts from thinking about things action-by-action, to thinking project-by-project. So whereas the first couple of stages are about getting up to date and paying attention to the detail, this stage is where you become a bit more of a visionary, and think ahead, with more of a view of the big picture. Even just for this single stage of a Weekly Checklist alone, you'll see why a Projects List really is such a vital tool!

▶ Now you know everything new has been captured, go through the Projects List and think about each project in turn. What do you need to be working on over the next week? What are the next physical actions? This is really important, because often what shouts the loudest from your email or social media isn't the most important stuff!

▶ Think about what else is happening in the 'wider world'. What are your friends working on? Are they starting to talk about dissertations and you're barely sure what one is? Are they arranging exam study groups? Do you need to start thinking about summer jobs or opportunities?

▶ What's the stuff you need to be doing that your course tutors won't 'spoon-feed' you?

Stage 4 – Practical Preparedness

This stage is about preparing for the battle, and avoiding stress later by actually getting some of those small details sorted out. This is your chance to do the slightly boring or tedious stuff that if you're not naturally organized (as I'm not!) you might be tempted to skip.

▶ Do I know where I need to be each day next week? (Checking lecture rooms or new locations on maps is much easier if you batch it up and think about it once a week when you're not lost and five minutes late for a class – something I learned the hard way, unfortunately!)

▶ Can I book tickets for travel in advance?

▶ Is there any printing I need for next week? (Do it now, and add it to your bag/file.)

▶ What books do I need from the library? (Think ahead here, especially for core texts that are likely to be in high demand!)

▶ What resources do I need to download? (Again, doing these things when you're not stressed is much easier, and doing them in bulk by batching them together saves loads of time, too.)

▶ 'Do' my bag for the week. (Get all the physical stuff you need ready, so for the rest of the week you don't need to think about this too much.)

▶ Prepare my gym kit/washing/ironing and any other chores.

Stage 5 – Questions

Much like the Daily Ritual, this is an opportunity for you to be your own coach: to use a little bit of Ninja Mindfulness to notice how you're thinking. This stage is particularly useful for making sure good habits stick (although actually all five stages will give you a great opportunity to reflect and make changes). Your questions can be deep or relatively shallow, big or small, specific or general. It doesn't really matter, as long as you feel they're helpful. But the bottom line is that spending just a few short moments each week asking yourself good questions is a powerful tool for self-development, reducing procrastination, being in tune with your intentions and feeling confident that you're on the right track. Remember these questions here are just suggestions. You can choose all of them or none of them. Ideally, choose some of these and make up a few of your own, depending on what you're most keen to keep an eye on.

Balance questions

▶ How's home?

▶ Am I nurturing my close relationships, or neglecting them? Is there anything I should do differently?

▶ How can I be kind to others this week?

▶ How can I be kind to myself?

▶ Did I do my fair share of the cooking and washing up? And if not, how can I make it up to everyone else?!

Zen-like Calm questions

▶ Now that I've done the rest of this Weekly Checklist, do I feel ready for the next seven days?

▶ Are there any nagging stresses, shiny new ideas or things that seem unclear?

Ruthlessness questions

▶ What can I say no to from my list?

▶ What do I need to say no to in the rest of my life?

▶ What can I delete from my lists?

▶ What could I delegate to someone else, or 'piggyback' on (can I ask a friend if I missed the lecture, can we chip in together to sort birthday presents to save me doing it alone, etc)?

Weapon-savvy questions

▶ How well is my Second Brain working?

▶ How well is the app, paper system or whatever other Second Brain tool I'm using actually working for me? Do I need to solve any problems or issues so that I trust it more?

Focus questions

▶ Is there anything on my Master Actions List that's really too big?

▶ When are my big opportunities to make progress next week? On which days do I have blocks of proactive attention, and what is so vital it needs scheduling in one of those blocks, to ensure I have Focus on it?

▶ What can I do to avoid interruptions?

Mindfulness questions

▶ Are there actions that I know are important but I'm resisting? (Remember, think DUST: Are they Difficult, Undefined, Scary or Tedious?) What can I do to change how I think about each of these?

▶ How do I feel?

▶ What thoughts are most often running through my mind, either now as I do this Checklist review, or during the week as a whole?

Preparedness and health questions

▶ Am I sleeping well?

▶ Am I eating well and drinking enough water?

▶ Am I exercising?

▶ Did I meditate or practise yoga this week?

Human questions

▶ What went well last week?

▶ What can I learn from the last week?

▶ If I were being more realistic with myself about what's achievable next week, what commitment would I drop, postpone or change?

▶ What Ninja characteristic do I need more of next week?

So that's the five stages of a Weekly Checklist. The aim is to reach a level of trust in the Second Brain that means you can spend most of your week without even needing to think about your projects – you're just calmly following your Master Actions List and safe in the knowledge that you're doing what really matters. It will take a bit of practice, but once you master this habit, everything else we've been talking about so far will fall into place – and the Weekly Checklist really is the glue that holds is all together.

WHEN, WHERE AND HOW LONG?

In general, it's worth setting aside an hour or even 90 minutes each week to complete the Weekly Checklist. You may find – particularly if you don't have a huge number of projects and actions on those main lists – that it's more like 30–45 minutes. But having 90 minutes set aside means you're not rushing, and those questions at the end are, I think, the most critical part of making the whole process a success, so you don't want to be rushing at the end because you're out the door to a class.

The best places to sit and review your entire world (which is really what the checklist is there to help you do!), are places where you have access to your stuff but there's a low level of distraction. Perhaps somewhere that feels like a treat, or a nice place to think. I know people who do theirs in their favourite coffee shop and treat themselves to a piece of cake while they do it, or choose a particular room in the house, or somewhere where you can gaze out at an interesting or inspiring view. For many years, I did a lot of mine on trains, as I spent most weekends travelling from Brighton to watch my football team, Aston Villa, some 350 miles away, so I had a lot of time to kill! Plus, the lack of wifi, Virgin trains' coffee and the rolling hills helped my thinking. These days my son is on the train with me, so it's no longer the best time.

And then there's the question of what time in the week. Again, there's no right and wrong here, but choosing a time when you'll have access to a good level of proactive attention – doing the Weekly Checklist properly will force you into some of the hardest thinking in your whole week – and of course minimizing distractions matters. So in the middle of the dining table in the front room with the TV on and everyone coming in and out isn't the best idea. Find a bit of Stealth and Camouflage. Hide yourself away so that you can do some quality thinking.

If there's a particular day when you know you're generally home alone, or have a quieter period of time, do it then. Some people doing this in work settings love Mondays or Fridays because it gives either a sense of focus to kick-start the week, or a sense of closure to bring the week to an end and get ready for the next one. Both of these options mean people enjoy their weekends more, so who is anyone to argue with that!

EXERCISE: WEEKLY CHECKLIST

Now it's time for you to develop your own Weekly Checklist. The five stages are listed below. Simply go back through the example suggestions and decide what you think you should adopt for your own checklist, and what you don't need – and feel totally free to add in your own ideas, too. Make this yours. And remember the Ninja principle of Human, not Superhero: you won't get this perfect first time, and that's totally fine. You're not looking for perfection here, you're looking for a great start. You will inevitably want to update and change what's on your checklist once you've had a couple of weeks of experience using it. You can also find a downloadable PDF resource to help with this, at: www.studyninja.online/resources

Stage 1 – What's new?

_____

_____

_____

_____

_____

_____

_____

_____

_____

_____

_____

_____

Stage 2 – Get your Second Brain up to date

_____

_____

_____

_____

_____

_____

_____

_____

_____

_____

_____

_____

_____

Stage 3 – Think ahead

_____

_____

_____

_____

_____

_____

_____

_____

_____

_____

_____

_____

_____

_____

Stage 4 – Practical Preparedness

_____

_____

_____

_____

_____

_____

_____

_____

_____

_____

Stage 5 – Questions

Balance questions

_____

_____

_____

Zen-like Calm questions

_____

_____

_____

Ruthlessness questions

_____

_____

_____

Weapon-savvy questions

_____

_____

_____

Focus questions

_____

_____

_____

Mindfulness questions

_____

_____

_____

_____

Preparedness and health questions

_____

_____

_____

Human questions

_____

_____

_____

TERMLY RITUALS

If you're studying with an institution that works in terms (or half-terms, or semesters), then it's probably also worth giving some thought to what each one is about. I'll refer to them as 'terms' for the rest of this bit, but the same principles apply even if you use a different word other than 'term'.

In truth, the design of the journey through your learning, from the age of four or five right through to post-graduate or adult learning, is exactly that: designed. Each term or year is designed to build on the previous one. The journey all the way through school is as much a journey towards your individual independence as it is an academic journey. Each year the expectations of you are higher, you're taking on more responsibility for your 'stuff' and you're gradually honing things about your own learning, such as the subjects you enjoy, the way you like to learn, your habits and so on. As you go through degree study and post-graduate study, if you get that far, it's expected that you're responsible for your life outside of study, but the independence of your learning also grows: it's less about being dictated to and more about you setting your own directions for learning and research.

So with this in mind, it's worth knowing at the start of each year and the start of each term what the 'game' is: are you facing a term where you're being asked to settle in and get used to new ways of working, or is this the term where the preparation needs to pay off in exam performance scores? At every stage, there's a game, and while some of those games have scores at the end and it's easy to know how well you've done, some games are more hidden – don't forget that teachers, schools and learning institutions all have bosses and performance targets of their own and expectations of you outside of your test scores. You'll also have expectations of yourself – both in terms of how you manage your learning and how you practise your Ninja Balance.

So the point of a termly checklist might be to look at this relationship from both sides, looking at:

Reflection:

▶ How was the last term?

▶ Reflect on average grades (and where you sit alongside everyone else) – but don't get grade envy!

▶ What do I need to do differently?

▶ What momentum or excitement do I need to keep going?

My purpose:

▶ Revisit your purpose: why am I doing this anyway?

▶ Defining success: what would a successful next term look like?

Planning ahead:

▶ What do I expect of myself?

▶ What do *they* expect of me? How do I play the game? What help can I get?

Balance:

▶ What would a typical week this term look like?

▶ When do I have time for other things, outside of learning?

▶ When are my 'fallow periods' likely to be?

▶ Which weeks will be a nightmare and crazily busy?

▶ What are the natural milestone moments (half-terms, reading weeks, big personal events) and what do I want to prioritize to have done before these milestones vs what can wait until after them?

Hobbies, activities, 'life':

▶ What do I need to sign up for or organize in advance?

Ninja Cheats

▶ If you don't have time to be organized right now, just sit down with a pen and paper and write down all the things you're working on. Getting all of the things that might be nagging you or inspiring you out of your head and onto paper will make you feel more in control of it.

▶ If you don't always have time to go through a Daily or Weekly Checklist, skip it, but be clear with yourself about the first date you're going to restart it. Knowing that there's organizational light at the end of the tunnel will allow you to muddle through until then.

▶ When you're under the pressure of deadlines, focus on maintaining your organizational systems, and when the pressure is off, that's the time to review and update your systems.

Are you a Study Ninja?

▶ A Study Ninja develops Zen-like Calm by being organized and in control.

▶ A Study Ninja knows the importance of Preparedness, both to stay sane and to identify potential time-savings and efficiencies.

▶ A Study Ninja develops Focus by being clear about how long each task will take and the levels of their attention needed to make things happen.

3. MASTERING NINJA BALANCE

HOW TO MANAGE YOURSELF, THE SCIENCE OF MAKING BETTER DECISIONS AND HOW TO HACK YOUR BRAIN

In the last chapter we talked about scaffolding, structures and the things you need to do to ensure maximum efficiency and to achieve sure-fire Study Ninja status. All of what we've discussed so far, fitted together, is like the perfect machine for producing the perfect academic performance. Turn the handle of the machine, watch the magic happen. Now, I have good news and bad news.

> The good news is this: all you need to do now is turn the handle of that machine.

> The bad news is this: all you need to do now is turn the handle of that machine.

A Study Ninja is a human being, with fantastic gadgets, habits and skills. But a Study Ninja is not a superhero with special powers who can magically put this all into practice without any effort or hiccups along the way, and navigating these is probably the biggest obstacle to academic success.

WHY YOU'RE DEFINITELY WRONG.

Perhaps you've reached this stage of the book thinking: 'This is all just common sense, I do all this already.' If so, then you're wrong. Common sense, yes I'll give you that. Consistently or even commonly applied? Hell, no! No-one I know or have ever coached has this stuff fully mastered, and I certainly don't either. There's always room for improvement and we all have a lot to learn.

But perhaps you've actually reached this stage of the book thinking: 'This all seems so difficult, so pie in the sky, so beyond my capabilities.' If so, then you're wrong too. Perfection is indeed beyond you (because it's beyond all of us) but getting *really* good at all this stuff is much easier than you think.

WHY WE'RE ALL WRONG, MOST OF THE TIME.

The way we think, act and decide on things is generally wrong. We all think we're smarter and less prone to bad thinking or bad decision-making than everyone else, but the truth is no-one is immune. In this chapter, I'll show you some of the science that proves that the way we think is wrong. We'll look at some of the common mistakes our brains make and some of the ridiculous biased thinking that sets us up to fail time and time again. Self-help 'gurus' will tell you that building a successful, balanced life is all just a question of planning, or visualizing, or buying their expensive coaching programme to help you get rich, get laid and get beautiful. But even if what they were selling was all true (!), the question of balance is often laid out as one that's ultimately about planning or emotional intelligence: get in touch with your feelings or plan out your goals and then *let the magic happen*. Rarely do any of those people ever tell you what a lousy and irrational brain you have, and show you the trip wires laid out in front of you on the magical journey they promise. So I'm not promising life-changing perfection, but what I am promising is a map to help you negotiate the pitfalls you'll encounter on your way to Ninja Balance.

THE GRASS IS ALWAYS GREENER

An example of what makes Balance difficult to achieve is the old adage that 'the grass is always greener on the other side'. If we're spending too much time socializing, we envy those with the discipline to study harder. When we've got our noses buried in a book, we're jealous of those who are sat relaxing, drinking and having fun outside. This is something I experience most days in summer, living in a seaside town and riding to work along the seafront promenade. And yet I have no boss, so why don't I just take the day off, stop working so hard and spend the day on the beach? Well, over the years I've got better at knowing when it's OK to do just that. Because sometimes, Ninja Balance IS about skipping work and enjoying the sunshine. But sometimes it's about skipping sunshine and making sure I'm enjoying work.

LAZY, SCATTERBRAINED YOU VS CLEVER, MOTIVATED YOU

Have you ever noticed how sometimes you're practically a genius, with everything in perfect balance and harmony, and yet other days you're an idiot, consciously avoiding the reading, writing or studying that's most important? We go from the 'Why am I such an IDIOT?' 'Why did I leave this so LATE?!' nightmares through to: 'I got the essay done a whole day before the deadline. Smooooooth!', 'Look at me pressing "submit" ahead of time! Don't you worry world, I got this covered!'

Habits and self-discipline play a huge part in success. When I'm coaching people on productivity people often say to me: 'Isn't this all just about self-discipline?' My short answer is always: 'Well, nearly. But certainly once you have the right tools and know how to use them properly, then yes.' Of course, you need to have the resources and you need to know what you need to do to succeed. Beyond that, yes, it's really a question of self-discipline and being mindful and conscious of your own habits and intentions. Of course, this is one of those beautiful contradictions – it's both as easy and as difficult as that. We generally know what's good for us and what's not, and yet we don't always follow through in making the changes to our habits and behaviours.

It's a battle between the two different versions of you. In the red corner is the Clever, Motivated you. You want to get things done, you know what's healthy and what's not, you know what you need to avoid. However, in the blue corner is the Lazy, Scatterbrained you.

The Lazy, Scatterbrained you loves nothing more than gawping at YouTube for short-term gratification and forgetting all the important things. The Lazy, Scatterbrained you enjoys nothing more than lounging around doing absolutely nothing. There's no motivation and no will in this version of you – it will do anything for an easy life.

Your job as the Clever, Motivated you is to recognize that part of you is Lazy and Scatterbrained – and that, left to its own devices, this part of you will screw things up. So you have to 'trick' this part of you. You might do this already, by putting your library book in your bag the night before your class, so you don't forget to take it with you in the morning, or by setting elaborate alarms in your phone to remind you of everything you might forget. I've heard hundreds of stories of similar tricks, all of which boil down to your brain in Clever, Motivated mode taking some form of action to override the inevitable Lazy and Scatterbrained mode that's coming.

So you really have two choices here: to trust your own willpower and self-control to win out, or to realize that to change your habits and stay disciplined, you need to be a Ninja in battle. In the battle between the Clever, Motivated you and the Lazy, Scatterbrained you, you need to be proactive and seek out the opportunities to make a difference to your habits. Being smart just once can sometimes be enough to override a hundred Lazy decisions. For example, turning the wifi off *once* saves a hundred thoughts of 'shall I just check …?'; installing blocking software *once* saves every log on to Facebook until you override that software; making a commitment to someone else *once* produces hours of Ninja Focus in order to make that thing happen on time. Often just one simple burst of proactive, Clever, Motivated, disciplined or daring behaviour forces you into Ninja-level Focus that overrides hundreds of temptations for the Lazy, Scatterbrained you for hours to come. And if you need any more convincing, let's look at some of the science behind some of the worst of our human thinking, and what you can do about it.

WHY MARSHMALLOWS HOLD THE KEY TO YOUR FUTURE HAPPINESS

The Lazy, Scatterbrained version of you wins out regularly and often. The idea of 'delayed gratification' is a great example of this. The famous 'Stanford Marshmallow Experiment' has been repeated and reconfirmed many times since it was originally conducted in the late 1960s by a psychologist called Walter Mischel at Stanford University. The experiment involved children sitting in a room being given a single marshmallow by a supervisor. They were then given two choices: eat the marshmallow over the next fifteen minutes, while the supervisor left the room, or wait until the supervisor returned, in which case they'd be rewarded with a second marshmallow.

You can almost hear the inner monologues of the Lazy, Scatterbrained you and the Clever, Motivated you as a child, in that scenario. The Clever, Motivated you is rationalizing: 'Well, I didn't have ANY marshmallows before I entered the room. If I hang on fifteen minutes, I'll have two!' And the louder, brasher, Lazy and Scatterbrained you, squealing and salivating with excitement: 'Oooh! A marshmallow! It looks so tasty! Let's eat it now! Whooooo!'

In follow-up studies with the same children later in life, the researchers found that the children who were able to wait longer for their double marshmallow reward tended to have better life outcomes, higher educational achievement, better body mass index scores and a whole host of other life success measures.

Equally, it was found that those who did not wait long and ate the marshmallow straight away were more likely to have behavioural problems, lower academic performance as teenagers, lower income and self-esteem as adults, and were even more likely to take drugs, be obese or get divorced.

When you think about it, the very idea of living a balanced life, in which you have the right focus on every area of your life, involves an awful lot of *not* focussing on areas – in other words, delaying gratification over your academic life in order to achieve gratification in your personal life, then switching that part to the background and achieving gratification somewhere else. The story of happiness is in many ways the story of serial neglect, as we focus on one area enough to make a difference, to the temporary detriment of everything else in that moment. Being comfortable in compartmentalizing things will help your Ninja Focus. And this is why you shouldn't be watching YouTube while you study.

FUN POINTS

Not sure if you can delay gratification? Worried you might be tempted to jump right into the Facebook void instead of exercising Ninja Focus? I'm going to give you a little self-management system that you can use to make sure that you stay motivated and recognize that delayed gratification doesn't mean *no* gratification, it just means your time for fun will come.

The system is called 'fun points'. For each hour of study, you're going to earn half a fun point, so two hours of studying will bring you one full fun point, and so on. Then, you're going to spend these fun points in whatever way you choose. Worried about whether to go on a big night out or stay in and read? Check if you have enough fun points! Feeling guilty about meeting your friend for coffee? Don't worry, you can check your fun points balance. Wondering how many hours to do in the library today? Depends on whether your plans for the rest of the week involve the spending of fun points or the earning of them.

Fun points are your guide to Ninja Balance. Using fun points, you'll start to see the bigger picture – and I suggest tallying your fun points over a week or a month, rather than just a day, in order to get the full effect.

In periods where you're putting in a lot of hours studying and it feels like life is devoid of any leisure, you can start planning how you're going to treat yourself to a fun point splurge when the deadline has passed. And in periods where you're spending a lot of time on relaxation, you'll at least know that your fun point bank account needs topping up with some serious reading sessions.

Here's a rough guide on how you could spend your fun points, but I've left some gaps here for you to write your own activities, too.

Number of Fun Points	How to spend them
1	One hour watching Netflix, messing around on the internet, etc.
2	Coffee with a friend
3	A dinner or a couple of quiet drinks, then home (the condition is no late night bleariness to deal with tomorrow)
6	A full-on night out, complete with stumbling home in the early hours and feeling a bit worse for wear the next morning
9	A whole day out/day off. Whether you spend it on rollercoasters, visiting your friend or sitting on your sofa drinking cups of tea is your decision. But it's a full day, dedicated to fun, relaxation, rest and … NO WORK.

Number of Fun Points	How to spend them

Since this is a mechanism for you to regulate yourself, I'm going to leave the small print down to you. So think about the following questions:

▶ Do you count all learning activities as earning fun points, or only the homework or self-directed study that happens 'off the timetable'? Doing the latter would of course mean tipping the balance slightly in favour of serious work and away from relaxation and fun, but that's your decision to make.

▶ Do hours spent doing work other than learning earn you fun points? You might decide that the part-time job that helps you pay your bills should earn you some more guilt-free downtime. Or again, perhaps you want to be more serious with your commitment to study time?

▶ Do you allow your fun points 'balance' to slip into overdraft? And if so, how many fun points is your limit? Be careful though, because just like with real money, borrowing fun points you haven't earned and spending them can become what you get used to, and a difficult habit to break.

▶ How do you draw the boundaries between time spent at home using fun points, and other downtime (for example, eating, showering, paying bills online, etc)? This is occasionally a bit of a grey area, but remember the purpose of fun points isn't to be a rigid system that you spend hours measuring, it's more a system by which you can include fun in your planning, but regulate the time you're spending in rest and relaxation mode.

EXERCISE: FUN POINTS

1. Draw up your own list of fun points prizes, using the table above as a starting point.

2. Put something in your diary or in your phone so that you can start to count your fun points over the next few days.

3. Think about what this system means for the time you've spent over the last week and any plans you've made for the next few days.

LEARNING AND IMPROVING SELF-CONTROL

We know it might be easier to self-manage ahead of time, but how can we improve our self-control in the moment? Well, scientific studies suggest you have more power over your self-control than you think, although as a resource it is limited.

A study led by the psychologist Mark Muraven in 1998 asked participants to regulate their emotions while they watched an upsetting movie. They then had to use a hand grip device to measure their physical stamina. When compared to a group who hadn't been asked to regulate their emotions, they were shown to have less physical strength and stamina. A different experiment asked people to write down whatever thoughts came into their heads, but some of the participants were then asked not to think about white bears. Of course, if I say to you 'don't think of white bears', what are you going to want to think about? So the scientists were looking to see the effects of this extra effort of trying to suppress the thought of a white bear. Afterwards, participants were asked to solve some anagram puzzles, but what they didn't realize was that the anagram puzzles were impossible. The participants who had been asked to suppress the thought of white bears gave up on the puzzle more quickly than those who were allowed to think freely. What this shows is that there's only so much self-control in our brains at any one time – it is a finite resource, so we have to use it carefully.

This perhaps explains why people come in grumpy from a long day at work: they've spent all day exercising self-control, and when they get home they know they have the freedom to do and say whatever they like, without the same judgement or consequence as at work! You might want to bear this in mind when thinking about the balance between personal relationships and periods of intense study. Roy Baumeister, one of the most renowned psychologists working in this area, calls this 'ego depletion'. So in effect, each piece of effort depletes your reserves of self-control that little bit more, and slowly wears you out (think about the argument you had at home last week after a day of regimented self-control). And, knowing this, think about the best and worst times to schedule difficult conversations in the future, if you have any choice over this!

TAKING YOUR SELF-CONTROL TO THE GYM

While it might feel from reading that last bit like you've just been doomed to failure by science, Baumeister's work on 'strength control' also suggests that you can treat self-control as a muscle which you can develop over time, like any other. So while our levels of self-control do deplete, we can also increase our levels by working the muscle like we would any other. Baumeister has also shown that exercising self-control makes links between unrelated areas. So for example, if you can perfect a controlled behaviour in one area of life, such as regularly getting up at the same time, this leads to a form of resistance to the 'ego depletion', and you're more likely to be able to, say, run home from the library every day too.

Your self-control is like any other muscle: overuse it and it gets tired, but build it up slowly and you'll get stronger with each day. If you think about your self-control in this way, it pays to spread out those difficult tasks throughout the day or week, just as, if you had to train for a marathon, you'd gradually build up the number of miles you run as you get fitter and your leg muscles develop.

Finally, this is also why educational institutions and workplaces schedule in regular holiday breaks (and why you should use them properly) and also shows the importance of allowing yourself a bit of Ninja Balance by taking breaks and not being too hard on yourself. It's important in developing any muscle to allow time for recharging and regrouping after periods of working out. Rest is, after all, a key tenet of Ninja Preparedness.

DECISION FATIGUE

Baumeister also links the thought processes that surround self-control with wider decision-making. He argues that that self-regulation includes not just controlling your behaviours, but also decision-making, exerting control, leadership of others, taking initiative, taking on responsibility, and so on. This view of self-regulation raises the possibility that the energy used in self-regulation may also be involved in other processes of the self's executive function.

In a 1998 study, participants were asked to make a long series of choices between products – or, in the control condition, simply to report on their usage of those same products. Afterwards both groups, with a new experimenter, were asked to drink a bad-tasting drink. The people who had been forced to make lots of choices were much less able to drink significant amounts of the drink, compared to the people in the control condition. So again, it's important to consider the issue of 'fatigue', in decision-making as well as self-control.

So if you're thinking that your job doesn't affect your studying and vice versa, it's worth looking closely at how you manage those 'reserves' of self-control. And if you're putting yourself in lots of stressful decision-making situations – whether that be moving house, writing an essay, co-ordinating a family event or answering lots of emails, it's worth noting that each of these things has an effect on the others.

Again, this shows the importance of Ninja Balance, of not being too hard on yourself and being realistic about what's achievable.

THE PLANNING FALLACY

It's often said that if you fail to plan, then you plan to fail. While this is certainly true, 'the Planning Fallacy' would also suggest that we wildly overestimate our own planning abilities; and in general, we wildly underestimate how long things take.

The most commonly cited example of the Planning Fallacy comes from a 1994 study conducted by academics from Simon Fraser University in British Columbia, in which final year university students were asked for realistic estimates as to when they would have their theses finished, along with optimistic and pessimistic estimates. The average actual time taken was 7.4 days longer than the 'pessimistic' estimate, 21.6 days longer than the 'realistic' one, and 28.1 more than the 'optimistic' one. This experiment is a prime example of how we overestimate our powers of planning and doing, but it's by no means a single case: tax form completion, computer programming, origami, furniture assembly – they've all been used in studies to demonstrate the Planning Fallacy.

There are two other 'laws' it's worth thinking about when it comes to planning – Parkinson's Law ('work expands to fill the time available') and Hoffstadter's Law ('work takes longer than you expect, even when you take into account Hoffstadter's Law'). And I don't mind admitting that overly ambitious planning is one of my own pet productivity weaknesses.

EXERCISE: 'EVEN WHEN YOU TAKE INTO ACCOUNT HOFFSTADTER'S LAW ...'

1. Think of something you have to start planning soon, such as an essay, a piece of coursework, a personal project or a work project.

2. Make an immediate estimate for how long you think it will take. Don't think about it too much, just write down whatever your brain or your gut comes up with first!

3. Now, take a few moments to think about how realistic that is. Think about the likely barriers you might face towards completion, or some of the things that might throw you off track. Think about similar tasks you've done and whether they ran over time.

4. Explore this a little further, remembering the Planning Fallacy, Parkinson's Law and Hoffstadter's Law.

5. Make a final estimation for how long it will take.

It's very natural that even when we know these kinds of laws exist, our brains still jump to breaking them. We tend to want to take quick decisions, and allow our future selves the smallest level of future pain possible, so we veer towards overly optimistic assumptions.

Now think about this for a moment. Everything in your life is subject to the Planning Fallacy. Everything. So what that ultimately means is that as human beings we constantly bite off more than we can really chew. What can you say no to today and what can you reassess, based on this?

COGNITIVE BIASES

Cognitive Biases describe things that our brain either chooses to ignore, or places too much emphasis on, skewing our thought processes. There are lots of examples:

THE ENDOWMENT EFFECT AND THE CURSE OF FLAT-PACK FURNITURE

The Endowment Effect suggests that we place more value on things that we own over things that we don't. One study found that owners of tickets for a high-profile basketball match overvalued them by a factor of fourteen. Most similar studies don't show such a high ratio as 14:1, but do point to there being a common problem in us over-valuing our own things. Think about all the clutter in our lives. Whether it's clothes that hold sentimental value even though they're worn out, or books that we favour in our work just because we didn't *buy* the other books, there are lots of ways in which our ownership dictates our relationship to things. Linked to this is what's known as 'The Ikea Effect'. You'll perhaps not be surprised to learn that this is the tendency for people to place a disproportionately high value on objects that they partially assembled themselves, such as furniture from Ikea, regardless of the quality of the end result. We might therefore see our own notes as more valuable than someone else's, just because we experienced making them ourselves, and equally we can become invested in certain decisions or ideas just because we experienced their creation. (This is especially true for writers – the edit process of a book involves hundreds of tiny funerals, as we let go of some of the ideas we spent a long time creating!)

ANCHORING

Anchoring, or 'focalism' as it's otherwise referred to in the cognitive psychology world, is another cognitive bias. It describes the common human tendency to rely too heavily on the first piece of information offered (the 'anchor') when making decisions. Once an anchor is set, other judgements are made by adjusting away from that anchor rather than evaluating each piece of new evidence on its own, so there is a bias towards interpreting other information around the anchor. This is why in so many scenarios, a first impression becomes so crucial. They say that the first year of a university course is for making friends and the remaining years are about shaking off most of them. And the same is true for our learning decisions: we may favour the part of the topic we started with all those months ago, rather than the one we've actually come to know the best.

CONFIRMATION BIAS

Confirmation bias describes the tendency for people to (consciously or unconsciously) seek out information that conforms to their pre-existing view points, and subsequently ignore information that goes against them, both positive and negative. If you think about how your political views inform your reading or consumption of the news, or how your impression of a particular company affects the approach you take to your next purchase (or boycott!) with them, you get the idea. Confirmation bias is a significant idea to consider in your learning and avoiding it is an important part of rationalism and of science in general. It also has ramifications for managing the rest of your life: imagine if you're in a conversation with a friend and you're asking them if you've upset them. The chances are that at some point in the conversation they'll tell you something like, 'it's OK', or, 'don't worry', as well as offering some words that hint at the opposite conclusion – that you have indeed upset them. Our brains use confirmation bias in this instance to pick out only the bit that we want to hear, and conveniently ignore any evidence to the contrary. Think about the way people argue about politics or religion on Twitter – the phrase 'I've never thought about it like that before, you've changed my mind' is oh so very rare! So constantly ask yourself if what you're concluding is down to an objective look at all the facts, or whether you're falling into confirmation bias.

Finally, being conscious of confirmation bias is a great tool for structuring arguments in essays, presentations and classroom debates. Try writing by rehearsing the entire argument from the opposite point of view to what you really think. For example, if your belief is that state-run healthcare institutions like the NHS are the most efficient way to deliver healthcare, try arguing for a completely free market with no state intervention whatsoever. Doing this probably won't make you change your mind, but it will help you expose any weaknesses in your own argument, which you may not otherwise be able to pinpoint. Occasionally you may choose to actually write the essay arguing an opposing view, which is a great way to develop academic rigour.

THE AVAILABILITY HEURISTIC

This is a cognitive bias where we tend to favour the information that we have available over and above information we don't have. For example, if I asked everyone in your house what percentage of washing dishes or cooking or household chores each person in the house did, most people would rate their own contribution as higher – and everyone else's lower – than it really is. This is because we remember doing the dishes on certain days, and even overestimate how many days we did them on, yet we underestimate the things that we don't see. In terms of studying this means that, if you come back from holidays having made very little progress with your coursework, for example, it's much easier to convince yourself this is fine if you don't have the available data about your friends' efforts.

THE BIAS BLIND-SPOT

Social Psychologist Emily Pronin and her co-authors did an experiment where they first explained to subjects a whole range of cognitive biases, including some of the ones above and others such as the 'better-than-average effect', where people are likely to see themselves as inaccurately 'better than average' for positive traits and 'less than average' for negative traits (everyone thinks they're a better than average driver; no-one describes themselves as a worse than average listener, for example).

Having just heard all the scientific research about biases, the subjects were then asked how biased *they* were themselves. Subjects still rated themselves as being much less vulnerable to those biases than the average person – so we're even biased about how biased we are!

WHAT CAN WE DO ABOUT ALL THIS? TEN BRAIN HACKS TO IMPROVE YOUR LEARNING AND BALANCE

No-one is immune from the failures of the human mind, but there are a few other tricks of the mind that can work in your favour. So if you want to keep your life in Balance, here are ten simple ways to think and act differently:

1. Make *them* believe in you

Attitude affects altitude. An experiment by Rosenthal and Jacobson, known as 'Pygmalion in the classroom' demonstrated that: 'when teachers expect students to do well and show intellectual growth, they do; when teachers do not have such expectations, performance and growth are diminished'.

This is the ultimate example of a self-fulfilling prophecy; and one that we'd do well to take heed of. It's perhaps also a contributing factor in why it's often said that you are as successful as the average of your five closest friends; and that if you want to be a millionaire, you should hang out with millionaires.

So you can use this technique to boost your learning in two different ways, depending on your situation:

1. Get your tutor to 'talk you up'. Talk to your tutors about your expected grades – and ask them to predict what they think you're capable of, if you really pushed yourself. Without them even knowing, what this has done is planted the idea in their minds (as well as yours, of course!) that they need to get you to that level. You see, teachers and tutors are professionals, with their

own human foibles and insecurities too, so they'll feel bad about themselves if they fail to deliver what they've just promised.

2. Get moved on. If you feel you're surrounded by people who are destined for lower grades than you, you need to do everything you can to either move to a different class, surrounded by people at least as smart as you (or preferably smarter!), or to seek out the teacher's attention as someone who believes they're better than the predicted grade that's set for them. Make them think about you differently, move on in their minds if you can't move on physically to a different class. Have them thinking: 'Well, most of these people are destined for a C grade, but I must get *that* person to an A – they're capable of it.' Remember, it's a self-fulfilling prophecy. Both you and the tutor will work harder to make it happen, even without them realizing why.

2. Make *you* believe in you

Linked to the above is another delicious piece of scientific discovery. One of Henry Ford's famous quotes echoes this study: 'Whether you think you can, or you think you can't, you're right.' Having belief in your own abilities genuinely helps bring about success. For a start, it motivates you and breeds momentum, so you're less likely to procrastinate and also means you're less likely to need significant self-control to get through the work. A famous Mischel and Staub study (yes, the same Mishel who did the marshmallow experiment) gave adolescent participants bogus positive or negative feedback for their performance on a series of verbal reasoning tests. The participants then had to make many choices, including one between a highly valued reward which they'd get for their successful performance on a similar reasoning task, or a less-preferred reward that they'd get regardless of their performance on the next test. As expected, individuals who had been primed to believe they would succeed through (false) positive feedback chose much more often to work for the reward than the ones who were primed for failure.

You may also have heard the phrase, 'fake it 'til you make it'. The truth is, out in the real world there are an awful lot of people who can get away with 'talking up' their skills and abilities because they have innate self-confidence. It's often months or years before the person who excelled in the job interview is found out to be a bit of a flake or a bit of a fake. In fact, more often, they soon learn what they need to do to fit in or survive. Most things in life are not that hard once you've had practice, so the power of self-belief actually trumps ability in many situations.

By the way, that fear you have about being 'found out', often known as 'imposter syndrome'? Most other people have it too, despite their outward appearances. So trust yourself. You're as good as them – all of them – and simply knowing this will help you succeed.

3. As you increase your achievement expectations, lower your to-do list expectations

As we saw with the Planning Fallacy, it's very easy to get caught up in a wave of enthusiasm and misplaced optimism about how long the assignment will take (and trust me, even knowing this, teaching this and researching this, I'm writing this with the deadline looming for this book!). So whenever you're planning, whether it's the timeline for a whole project or just what you plan to do for a one-hour free study period, go easy on yourself. Think of some ways to introduce constraint to your thinking, to temper enthusiasm. You'll remember I said I wrote my Daily To-Do List on a regular-sized Post-it note? Well, one of the benefits is that Post-its are quite small, so it forces me into the constraint of what can fit on that little piece of paper.

4. Think about your pea pods

And if you think it's impossible to increase your expectations about final grades while at the same time accepting that you can only do so much, there's a well-known rule of economics that can help. The Italian economist Pareto famously came up with Pareto's Law – also known as the rule of

80-20. He found this by looking around his garden and realizing that 20% of his pea pods produced 80% of his peas. The same principle can be applied in economics and business: companies like Apple, for example, will gain 80% of their profits from 20% of their activities (usually, for the last few years, particular models of the iPhone and iPad), whereas other companies might make 80% of their profits from 20% of their customers. The same is true for how wealth is spread in the world: roughly 20% of the world's population consume about 80% of the resources and have 80% of the wealth.

And here's the interesting bit. The same is true for you. That three hours you spent yesterday writing that essay? Probably 20% of that time was the time you were fully in Ninja Focus mode – 20% of the time produced 80% of what is good. And the more you start to realize this subtle but powerful rule, the more magical it becomes. With so many things you do, it's best to move on earlier than you realize. Reading research articles? Get the gist and move on quickly, don't linger. Brainstorming ideas for the assignment? Plan to do it in ten minutes instead of half an hour. Worried you should attend a friend's birthday party but can't afford a late night? Go for an hour and then disappear (choosing an hour carefully based on when your appearance will be most memorable but when it won't be rude to be seen to leave after an hour – I usually favour 'early but not too early' as my policy here!). Missed a one-hour lecture? Ask a friend to spend five minutes telling you the three or four key points.

The last moments we spend on things, where we're not quite ready to declare it 'perfect', are often the moments when we're stuck in Pareto's misplaced 80%: we rarely add the real essence of something right at the end. Usually we're just tinkering because we can't bear to let go. So let go of things as soon as you think they're *practically* finished, so that you can move more swiftly onto the next thing. (There are of course a few exceptions here, such as when you're working on assignments for the extremely pedantic, or the last twenty minutes of exams where extra moments mean extra marks and you really have nowhere else to be.)

5. **Plan in private ...**

A number of studies have suggested that the Planning Fallacy occurs more often and more potently in groups, and that often there's a tendency for people to be looking to impress the rest of the group by setting wildly unrealistic deadlines. Whether this is due to the need to impress other people by saying you can finish something quickly ('Look! A superhero!'), or whether it's down to what's often referred to in the business world as 'group-think' – where a group of people all start to think the same, and often will kid themselves that things are better than they really are by feeding on each other's enthusiasm – you can turn this around for yourself. Make plans for your own projects in private. If you're involved in group work, try to make your own version of a timeline before your group meets. Yes, you might look like a super-geek by turning up with a plan you've done already, but the chances are your private planning will be more realistic and will at least give the group something to think about.

6. **... but commit in public**

Public proclamations can often lead to bursts of extreme Ninja Focus. This is particularly useful when you feel like there's a task or project that will be susceptible to 'drift'; perhaps something that's not your top priority, but that equally you don't want hanging around too long. Realizing that your own motivation for completing it is perhaps little more than the thought that 'it'd be nice to get this out of the way', you need something bigger to motivate you. We're always happier letting ourselves down than we are letting other people down, so with that in mind, make a bold, external commitment to a family member, teacher, work colleague or someone else. Create public accountability. This should focus your mind to get it done, get it out of the way, and leave more time for you to have a life as well.

7. **Laugh and be generous**

Although it is not clear exactly how the mechanism functions, recent research has suggested that a positive mood helps to stop your levels of self-control from running out, while also allowing quicker replenishment. So laughter really is the best medicine for boosting self-control! Studies have also found that good mood has been induced through the giving of surprise gifts and the watching of comedy videos. This may seem like obvious advice, but it's worth remembering in those moments when you feel under pressure and a slave to the to-do list: keeping yourself happy helps to keep control, so a night out, some time with friends or just a couple of hours chilling on the sofa watching something that makes you giggle may actually all help you in the long run. The key here is to stop feeling so guilty about taking time off – see it instead as a positive contribution to Ninja Balance and Ninja Preparedness.

8. Drink lemonade

Willpower, it seems, is more than mere metaphor; it's a physical phenomenon too. In 2007, the psychologist Matthew Gailliot explored the role of glucose in the brain and in particular its relation to willpower. When glucose hits the bloodstream it can be converted to neurotransmitters, and thus becomes fuel for brain activity. Acts of self-control (like revision, or writing an essay) cause reductions in blood-glucose levels, which in turn predict poor self-control on behavioural tasks. Gailliot found that drinking a glass of lemonade with sugar helped counteract these effects, presumably because it's one of the fastest ways to restore glucose in the blood. Lemonade containing diet sweeteners (no glucose) had no such empowering effect. So if you're feeling low on energy and lacking self-control, a big glass of lemonade might actually save the day, and while it won't work wonders for your waistline, the occasional sugar rush can be good for a bit of a short-term energy booster, too!

9. **Never commit on a wave of enthusiasm**

My business coach, Rasheed Ogunlaru, is a wise and gentle soul. I meet with him once every few weeks for coffee and he helps me work out what the hell it is I'm supposed to be doing. I may arrive with a hundred questions, but I always leave with a piece of wisdom: something I can take away and use to make changes, or rearrange my choices, or think differently about something that was troubling me.

One of Rasheed's favourite sayings is 'never commit on a wave of enthusiasm'. You may be excited by your idea for an essay title or the prospect of starting a new project with someone, where the two of you take turns to get each other riled up, but the worst thing you can do is make the commitment to it before you'd had a chance to sleep on it or flesh out the details of precisely how much work you're signing up to. I know I'm often guilty of falling in love with the idea but then falling out of love with the practicalities. This is a key part of Ninja Ruthlessness: learn to say no to things more quickly, and in the heat of excited moments, always ask for time to think before you make a commitment. If the opportunity is that good, and it's meant to be, then it'll still be there in the morning.

10. **Avoid 'DDD'**

Distant Deadline Deficiency (DDD) is a term I've created to describe something I notice a lot in my work on productivity. I've given it a name, so that we can start to address it more honestly. It's the condition where a deadline feels too distant to motivate us, yet we feel like we should still be working towards it.

Picture this: You have a deadline in about a week. Guilt keeps you strapped to the desk, but you'd much rather be out having some fun or living the rest of your life. You persevere, trying to motivate yourself, but the deadline is too far off and you know deep down that it can *all* wait until tomorrow. There's zero consequence to drifting through the day or the evening, lightly checking a few texts in between YouTube videos and messages.

We tell ourselves, in the middle of this DDD, that there's some divine reason that we *should* be working, whereas do you know what you really *should* have done in that situation? Gone out and enjoyed your life! That's the 'should' created by a logical, reasoned and scientific view of the situation, rather than the one cooked up by your over-emotional inner monologue.

If you go out or spend a couple more days prioritizing other things, when you get a few days closer to the deadline and you're actually starting the assignment for real, you're doing so feeling fresh and ready to go. If instead you spend half a week chained to the desk out of guilt, making false sacrifices but getting nowhere, then what you've actually done is deplete your own self-control before you even start. So go out, have fun, relax. Know that it'll all happen when the deadline is shouting louder.

Parkinson's Law says that 'work expands to fill the time available', and this is so true for assignments and things with distant deadlines. If you're waiting until there are no deadlines before you stop sacrificing, you'll probably be waiting until the day you die. The point is to be motivated by other things, and to work optimally, play optimally, experience optimally, instead of being trapped by your coulds, shoulds and mights.

The same is true for an academic term or year: we tend to scan our calendars looking for the big deadline weeks and treat the rest of the time as some kind of hinterland. Ultimately, we need better ways to stay motivated other than just deadlines, and we need to draw firmer boundaries that allow us to have fun as well as work hard, to experience the joys of life outside of learning, which, rather counterintuitively, keeps learning itself joyful too.

We'll return to this idea in chapter five, which is all about studying in the day-to-day, without the magic pull of the immediate deadline to propel us into productive action.

EXERCISE: NINJA BALANCE

Take a few minutes to answer these questions, and then fill in the sentences below to make a plan ...

▶ What are some of the common mistakes I'm guilty of?

▶ What can I do to put these right?

▶ How can I be kinder to myself?

▶ What small things can I do differently?

Next week, I will adopt a more balanced approach to my life by ...

_____

_____

_____

For the rest of this term, I will avoid ...

_____

_____

_____

Long-term habits I'm working at changing are ...

_____

_____

_____

Ninja Cheats

▶ We're all prone to biased thinking, even about how biased we are. Remember this when making any key decision.

▶ The Planning Fallacy tells us that we wildly underestimate how long things take. If planning an assignment, write down how many hours or days you think this will take and then multiply it by 2.5.

▶ Don't have time to implement everything here yet? Read the 'fun points' section on page 101 and adopt that system in minutes. This will help you manage the boundaries and distribute your time and attention between learning and life.

Are you a Study Ninja?

▶ A Study Ninja practises Balance. Practice never quite means perfect, but a Study Ninja knows that's OK.

▶ A Study Ninja knows when to apply Focus and when to stop pushing their luck. A Ninja in constant battle loses in the end, so it's important to know your limits.

▶ A Study Ninja doesn't see socializing or leisure time as a bad thing, they see it as vital Ninja Preparedness, getting them ready for the battles ahead.

4. HOW YOU LEARN

WHAT KIND OF LEARNER ARE YOU?

Have you ever wondered what learning really is? We know there's work involved and that it's sometimes boring and sometimes exciting. We know that the end result is to achieve some kind of success, wisdom, knowledge, exam passes, happiness, job progression and whatever other outcomes you have in mind. But what's the process we use to get there? And how can we make it work for us? In this chapter, we're going to focus on a couple of theories, but most importantly, the focus is going to be on you.

Firstly, I'm interested in helping you get an idea about how you learn best. This will have an influence over how you use the rest of this book, as different techniques will be more effective or less effective.

LEARNING – JUST DO IT

David Kolb is one of the world's most respected learning theorists and psychologists. One of his most famous theories is the theory of 'Experiential Learning' – in other words, that we learn best by doing. The most famous aspect of Kolb's theory is his four-stage learning cycle, defined as 1. concrete experience, 2. reflective observation, 3. abstract conceptualization and 4. active experimentation. Essentially, we have an experience, we reflect on that experience, we start to conceptualize or think about the experiences in the abstract, then finally we test and experiment with what we've learned. So the four stages of Kolb's learning cycle, in simple terms are:

1. Experience

2. Reflect

3. Conceptualize

4. Experiment and test

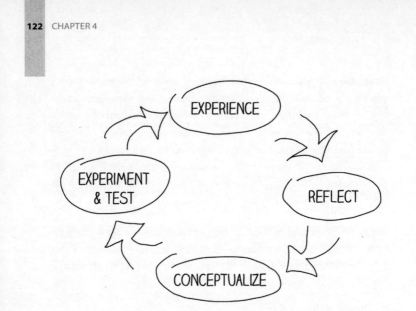

What Kolb is showing here is that learning is a process. It has a beginning, a middle and an end. And to learn effectively and sustainably means much more than just memorizing the answers for a test. As we look at these four stages in detail, I want you to think about your own learning experiences and see if you can identify moments where you've been engaged in each of these stages:

1. **Experience**

You experience a new situation or fact, or perhaps you come across something that you've seen or done before. As you encounter this, it's like being on a ship or a train with new horizons coming into view. You're anticipating what comes next, and you're driven by your emotions ('feeling' more than 'thinking'). So perhaps you're studying the history of Soviet Russia, and you're learning about the sense of hope felt by the people of Lenin's revolution or the despair of Stalin's era, or the pragmatism and transition of the Gorbachev era. You may be watching a film, or in a lecture or walking around a museum, but in whatever format, the information is new, or it's a new 'packaging' of things you'd heard about or read about before.

2. **Reflect**

After the experience you had, you're beginning to reflect on everything. You're starting to draw patterns in your mind between what you've just experienced and what you previously knew (if anything) about that topic. So perhaps you'd seen Lenin in a new light, or you're drawing comparisons between Stalin and other dictators like Hitler. Perhaps you're surprised by how much you felt the romanticism of the early revolutionary years, and that Lenin could be considered a 20th century visionary by some. Perhaps you're also reflecting on other more peripheral ideas, such as the significance for both Americans and Russians at that time of seeing McDonald's – a symbol of Western Capitalism – open their first restaurant in Moscow. Or perhaps you're wondering why anyone would queue to buy a Big Mac, or wondering how long you'd personally queue. Or beginning to feel hungry!

3. **Conceptualize**

As your mind makes the connections between what you experienced, your reflections lead – sometimes simultaneously, sometimes more slowly – to conclusions. You think about Stalin's dictatorship ('it seemed politically that Hitler and Stalin had such opposing ideologies and yet their methods and the consequences were similar …'; 'But wait a minute, Stalin fought alongside the British and against the Nazis in World War Two. Why was that?'), or you think about the hope that the people felt during the early stages of revolution and again during the tearing down of the Berlin Wall and the collapse of the Soviet Union. Maybe you create a bit of a theory in your mind that as long as politicians bring 'hope', it doesn't matter that much what kind of economic system they use to bring it about. And that 'hope' actually trumps 'reality'. You make other connections, too, such as the election of Barack Obama in the USA or Tony Blair in the UK.

4. **Experiment and test**

And finally with these new ideas, about what it means to be a leader, about what people vote for or favour above other things, about

McDonald's as a signifier of social progress, you look out for new experiences. You take these ideas and test them out. You bring them to bear when you're watching documentaries about Hugo Chavez or Mitt Romney, or when debating politics with your friends. Were you right or wrong? Do other experiences support your hypothesis, or lead you to question it further? Our brains in learning mode constantly seek new experiences to help us reassure ourselves or dismiss our assumptions as incorrect so that we can lead ourselves to something better. It's a cycle and a circle. It has no end-point as such.

Reading those four stages, what stood out to you? Which stage seemed the most powerful to you? Which one awoke your sense of excitement and most vividly took you back to experience of learning that you've had in the past? Where did you feel most at home? Was it in experiencing those new things and feeling excited about what's coming next? Was it in being able to quietly reflect on experiences and understand what you've experienced in a new way? Was it in taking that understanding and creating the hypotheses? Or were you most at home thinking about how you experiment and test and challenge what you think you know?

This is an important question to ask, because the chances are this is part of your own individual 'learning style'.

HEALTH WARNING TIME

It's important to say that these things are just a guide. It's a bit like when you do quizzes in magazines: it's not designed to be a definitive system and the truth is everyone can learn in each of the four styles, it's just you may have a preference. But it does give you some insight into the process of learning – which parts of it bring you to life and how you might exploit that to boost your learning. In other words, use these ideas as a guide, but don't take it too seriously. You can, however, take it more seriously than the 'Which city should I live in?' quiz that you took on Buzzfeed. I saw you. Please stop doing that, it only encourages them.

The other thing to say about learning styles and personality types is that there are so many different models, or ways to look at them. A couple of the most famous used professionally are Honey and Mumford's learning styles model (which actually uses Kolb's learning cycle model as its basis) and you might also have heard of the 'Myers-Briggs Type Indicator' (MBTI) where people start describing their whole personalities in groups of four letters, saying things like: 'that's because I'm an ESFP.' And everyone nods profoundly pretending they understand what that means, while they try to remember in the darkest depths of their brains what 'J' stands for and what their own letters were when they did the quiz three years ago on a management course. For years, I have remembered my own ('INTJ') purely because Richard Branson is ('ENTJ'), and for ages I thought we were the same. But then I realized that that one difference – my 'I' instead of his 'E' – stands for 'introvert' versus 'extrovert', and Richard Branson's extroversion is actually a huge part of his success. So I'm screwed, basically.

Well, no. And this is the problem with such categorizations. They often lead to limiting beliefs, as people label themselves or other people as one thing but not another thing, capable of learning in one scenario but they may as well write off their chances of learning a different way. So while these categorizations are great tools to gain a bit of understanding, to help see learning as a process, to help work out what your preferences might be, just remember that they should always be taken with a pinch of salt.

OK, health warning over. Let's do a bloody quiz, shall we?!

AURAL, VISUAL OR KINAESTHETIC?

One of the most common models of learning styles is the 'VAK' or 'VARK' model. The 'VAK' model has been used in the teaching of teachers and trainers for a long time and describes three particular learning styles:

Visual learners. They are at their best when they can 'see' what they're learning, so have a preference for pictures; visual aids, graphs, charts, diagrams and symbols. If you're a visual learner you may learn words best by remembering the layout of where you see them on a page of revision notes, for example, or by seeing those words in some kind of diagram.

Auditory learners. They learn best through listening to things – through lectures and discussions that bring the words to life. If you're an auditory learner you might remember words best by reading them out loud or by committing them to a song or poem.

Kinaesthetic learners. These people prefer to learn via the lived experience, such as moving, touching and doing, and through the active exploration of the world, experimentation with ideas and so on. If you're a kinaesthetic learner, you will respond best to learning where you're immersed or involved in the process, whether that means visiting a museum, conducting active experiments or simply making your own notes.

Any good teacher or tutor will be aware that their lessons should help students to learn in the way they find easiest (although, again, no single person only learns in one of these ways, it's about being more or less inclined to each, not an 'either/or' decision to only learn one way). The same is true for adult learning. My company, Think Productive, teaches workshops on productivity in businesses around the world. We spend a lot of time and effort thinking about the quality of the learning experience. I am always delighted when I read the evaluation forms and see that the scores are consistently high, but you might be surprised to learn that I'm even more pleased to see the occasional criticism: 'this bit was too long', or 'this bit needed more time for reflection'. Often we'll have two negative comments about the same thing that are completely contradictory – for example, one person saying the length of the workshops could have been an hour instead of three and another person saying they wanted the whole day instead of just three hours! What these kind of comments prove is that everyone learns in different ways – we're all beautifully different and human.

You will often hear this model talked about as 'VARK' instead of 'VAK', because Neil Fleming, a teacher from New Zealand, developed the model further. Basically, he split up the 'Visual' learner definition, redefining 'Visual' as mainly about pictures and graphs and adding a 'Reading and Writing' category. Neither is right or wrong, so for the purposes of the rest of this book, we'll stick with the original 'VAK' model, but if words are your thing, you might fit into the visual learner category after all.

What kind of learner are you? Time for a short quiz.

VISUAL LEARNERS
Visual learners learn best by seeing. Graphic displays such as charts, diagrams, illustrations, handouts, and videos are all helpful learning tools for visual learners. People who prefer this type of learning would rather see information presented in a visual rather than in written form.

If you think you might be a visual learner, answer the following questions:

Do you have to see information in order to remember it? ❏

Do you pay close attention to body language? ❏

Are art, beauty and aesthetics important to you? ❏

Does visualizing information in your mind help you remember it better? ❏

If you can answer yes to most of these questions, chances are good that you have a visual learning style.

AURAL LEARNERS

Aural (or auditory) learners learn best by hearing information. They tend to get a great deal out of lectures and are good at remembering things they are told.

Are you an auditory learner? Consider the following questions:

Do you prefer to listen to lectures rather than reading from the textbook? ❏

Does reading out loud help you remember information better? ❏

Would you prefer to listen to a recording of your lectures or a podcast rather than going over your notes? ❏

Do you create songs to help you remember information? ❏

If you answered yes to most of these questions, then you are probably an auditory learner.

KINAESTHETIC LEARNERS

Kinaesthetic (or tactile) learners learn best by touching and doing. Hands-on experience is important to kinaesthetic learners.

Not sure if you're a kinaesthetic learner? Answer these questions to find out:

Do you enjoy performing tasks that involve directly manipulating objects and materials? ❏

Is it difficult for you to sit still for long periods of time? ❑

Are you good at applied activities such as painting, cooking, mechanics, sports, and woodworking? ❑

Do you have to actually practise doing something in order to learn it? ❑

If you responded yes to these questions, then you are most likely a kinaesthetic learner.

Are you a Study Ninja?

▶ A Study Ninja is Weapon-savvy about their learning styles and chooses tools and techniques that fit with this style.

▶ A Study Ninja regularly reminds themselves that they're a Human, not a Superhero, which means they acknowledge their limitations, experiment to learn new skills, but don't fret if they encounter techniques that don't suit them.

▶ A Study Ninja is Prepared for action, and works on developing their generic learning skills in times when they're not under pressure.

5. GENERAL STUDY

STUDY

LEARNING DAY BY DAY

In this chapter and in the next three, we're going to look more practically at the core skills of learning: general day-to-day learning in this chapter, followed by writing, memory and revision techniques for exam study in the next chapter, and then finally exam performance in chapter seven.

When we look back at the end of any academic course, or at the end of any year or term, we reflect on our progress based on the test scores or overall grades. We are biased (psychologically, but I think as a society too) to only think about the destination rather than the journey. It is because of this that we tend to quickly forget what happens on the 80% of days when we're not being formally tested: the days where there are no assignments to hand in, you're not sat in an exam and you're just freely carrying on with your education, and more than likely carrying on with your life, too.

We tend to overlook the importance of these days. It might be our performance in the test that produced the score, but it was the preparation and day-to-day habits that led up to that point that were critical to the success. So, let's look a little bit more at these 'everyday' study days, and the obstacles you might encounter.

GETTING OUT OF BED

It's a cliché that students find it difficult to get out of bed. You may say that's because it's true, or you might be learning at a different stage of your life, where your own children are forcing you out of bed early in the morning. Either way, when there's no looming deadline, motivation is an issue. Why roll out of bed or pull yourself away from the rest of your life to study? There's no test to revise for, no assignment to prepare for and it's easy to convince yourself that the 'real work' is far, far away in a distant land. Football pundits often describe the final weeks of the season as 'the business end', and it can be tempting to tell yourself you'll raise your game for the cup finals, but just coast along week-to-week for the rest of the year.

DON'T BE NAKED: THE ART OF 'DAY-TO-DAY MAGIC'

To manage our studies well in the everyday, we need to change our focus. Expecting to cram and pull through, turn on the style when the assignments kick in, suddenly find an extra gear, magically put the rest of your life on hold ... while all of these are possible, they're by no means sure-fire bets – and none

of them will make you a better learner. A Ninja concentrates instead on Preparedness: the practical things that have you arriving at the exam hall not only having done the requisite level of revision, but feeling calm, rested and even a little smug. It's like arriving for the exam with every possible weapon at your disposal, ready to kick some ass. Now, do you want to turn up prepared, or do you want to turn up naked?

Creating what I call the 'day-to-day magic' is about slowly, piece by piece, building up the knowledge base you need for when the time comes. Exams and assignments are stressful enough, so to be approaching them unprepared or even badly prepared only adds stress. And to be deliberately using cramming or last-minute midnight oil-burning as a *strategy*? Not clever. In fact, when it comes to memory, psychologists talk about the 'spacing effect', which says that information absorbed over a longer period of time is remembered better.

Have *I* written things at the last minute and crammed for exams? Of course I have. (Confession: if you see me giving a talk and you hear me say it's the first time I've given that talk, I'll guarantee you I was still tinkering with the slides less than half an hour ago. I continue to figure out ways to avoid this, but it's one of the few habits I've been relentlessly pushing against with almost zero progress!) But I never said I was perfect. So in this chapter we'll look at the right way to create 'day-to-day magic', but we'll also spend some time looking at what to do when you *choose* to do something else – because it *is* a choice.

STAYING MOTIVATED ...

If we presume that there are at least some days when it's possible to be motivated by the quiet and conceptual promised land of our future success, rather than the shrill siren of an impending deadline, then those days are likely to be the ones where we're most connected to our intentions and purpose.

What is your purpose for learning? You might want to revisit the exercise we did earlier in the book – in fact, this is an exercise you can do regularly when you need some motivation. Spending a few moments contemplating that is a way to reconnect with your intentions and feel that what you plan to do that day does have a point. It's about recognizing that the battle for a Study Ninja is won in the preparation, even if the devastating blow is struck in the heat of battle. A Ninja uses Mindfulness and self-awareness to reconnect with their own motivations.

KICKING YOURSELF OUT OF BED

Of course there are the days when no amount of Mindfulness or self-efficacy will trump watching trashy daytime TV, or overcome your addiction to Snapchat. So in those circumstances, how do you get the day started and get motivated when there's seemingly no motivation in the tanks? Here are some suggestions for better alarm clocks ...

1. *Maths Alarm Clock*

If you suffer from continuously hitting the snooze button in the morning, the Maths Alarm Clock app makes you solve a simple maths problem in order to turn your alarm off. As well as the obvious benefit of making sure you're properly awake before it'll turn
itself off, it also gets your brain working first thing in the morning, which just might help kick-start your morning routine.

2. Keep your alarm clock in another room

For years, I had a really loud alarm clock, which I placed in the kitchen, next door to my bedroom. I knew that on the other side of that kitchen wall was my neighbour's kitchen, so if the alarm went off repeatedly, it was likely to disturb them. Within a few weeks of doing this, I would magically wake up about three minutes before the alarm was due to go off, and if I had a moment of relapse, I'd soon be woken by the alarm bellowing away three minutes later!

3. *Snappy days*

If mathematical problems or waking up the neighbours are not enough to get you out of bed, here's an even weirder solution: with the Alarmy app, you'll have to get out of bed and take a picture of your sink (or any other area you define) to turn off the alarm!

4. Rude awakening

Every smartphone has two apps that are rarely used together – an alarm clock, and a sound recorder. So allow the Clever, Motivated you to meet the Lazy, Scatterbrained you, first thing in the morning! In the middle of the day, record a couple of different greetings, or as many as you like, and then add these to your phone's alarm clock. Here are some suggestions:

'Get up you lazy b@st*d! NOW!'

'Good morning. On Saturday you may press snooze and have a lie-in, but for today, there's work to do. Breakfast is downstairs.'

'Good morning. Tell me: What are your intentions for today?'

'Get up! Don't think! Put your running shoes on! It's time to go running! Don't think! Get out of bed and go running!'

(set on another alarm for 20 minutes later) 'You lazy, lazy man. You disgust me. Get out of bed.'

5. Automatic aromas

If you prefer the proverbial carrot to the proverbial stick, get yourself a coffee maker with an automatic timer. Set the coffee maker to start brewing you fresh coffee half an hour before you want to get up. Then, let the aromas entice you out of bed and into the kitchen to pour yourself a nice warm welcome to the day.

Sleep Cycle

Sleep Cycle is a great little app for Android and Apple to help you manage your sleep. It works by putting your phone on the corner of your pillow and measuring the movements in the bed to analyse your sleep cycles, recognizing when you're in deep sleep, when you're in light sleep and when you're awake. Using this data, it can do really clever things like choose the perfect time within the parameters you set to wake you up. The idea is that you will feel much more refreshed if you wake at the end of a natural cycle of sleep, rather than letting a harsh alarm interrupt you in the middle of deep sleep. It also shows you graphs of your sleep and is a great tool to help develop Ninja Mindfulness by making you more conscious of how you look after your sleep.

STUCK IN THE MIDDLE WITH GUILT

When there's no deadline looming, you can either choose to kick into gear anyway, mindful that creating that day-to-day magic is more important than anything you create in an assignment or exam, or you can choose to kick back and enjoy the day. Finding a few days to do this is actually a really good thing – it promotes the Ninja Balance and

Ninja Preparedness that we need for successful study and a happy life. The trouble is, we often don't quite get to that decision. Instead of making the conscious decision to do one of those two positive things, we do something else: we beat ourselves up with guilt.

Guilt is a terrible emotion. While you can sometimes use a dose of guilt to spring yourself out of bed in the morning, to go through hours and hours of it while sat at your desk knowing you should be working on something constructive, but never reaching the point of deciding to give up for the day and relax instead, is completely pointless. It erodes your trust in yourself, it diminishes your self-esteem and it lowers your self-control and motivation levels further. Here's our typical behaviour hierarchy – not what we *should* do, but what we usually end up doing.

1. Ideally, we spend the day working on what's important (Ninja Focus). Well done us.

2. If that's not happening, we spend the day soldiering on, trying to kick into gear and reach Ninja Focus (but beating yourself up with guilt as we do).

Only occasionally do we choose to be bolder and notice which way the tide is flowing, give up and spend the day relaxing and having fun (achieving some Ninja Balance). But on a normal day we're trying to make some progress, but the guilt takes us to that place of 'DDD' that we discussed earlier. It's the guilt that keeps us locked into un-purposeful and ultimately unproductive and inefficient behaviour. Occasionally we *can* soldier on and break the cycle. But as a guide, how many times have you told yourself you'll soldier on and find a groove again, and how many times did it actually happen? As the American army general Colin Powell once said: 'Only the mediocre are always at their best.'

KNOW WHEN TO STOP

There's literally nothing good about spending a day caught in the middle between Ninja Focus and Ninja Balance. If you're in that mindset of saying, 'I'll just sit here and surf online for another twenty minutes, and then …', you're in danger of getting sucked into that vortex. If you're staring into space instead of staring at your revision notes, you're in danger, too. And if you're cancelling social plans and saying, 'No, I should probably try and do some reading tonight', you're in danger too. In fact, using words like 'probably' and 'should' are killer clues that you're not actually that committed this evening anyway – you can almost hear the guilt talking in your voice, before you've even 'failed'.

And do you know what would be best for you? Better than a whole evening in the guilt vortex and having achieved the grand total of ten minutes of Ninja Focus? A beer with your friends. Sometimes it's best to know when to say 'today isn't happening as planned' and go to the pub.

Of course, this isn't something you can do every day, but the point is you won't need to. Having time away from the work will help you. Your brain will think about other things, you'll start to relax, you'll get some perspective and most likely come back stronger tomorrow.

NINJA MINDFULNESS AND GUILT

Mindfulness in all its forms can be a great tool to combat guilt and DDD. Because ultimately, when you're trapped in that mode of DDD, what you really need is to notice your behaviour more quickly, and let logic rather than emotion rule the day. We tend to be driven by these  emotional desires that we're often not even that aware of. Noticing thoughts, patterns of behaviour and the ways in which you manage your own attention will go a long way to helping you stay out of the vortex. This leads us nicely on to managing our attention and boosting concentration.

PAYING ATTENTION

In day-to-day learning, the art of paying quality attention is vital. I'm not just talking about during lectures or classes here, either. Paying quality attention when you're quietly reading at home and even when you're out with friends is truly the most powerful gift you can give to yourself, as well as others. This is something I struggled with over the years. My attention in class would often be on the amusing 'game' we were playing to pass the time (such as daring each other to do things without the teacher noticing) rather than actually paying attention to the lesson. Sometimes this was justified – there's nothing more frustrating than a fascinating subject taught by a terrible teacher – but it's one of my very few regrets in life that there were gifted teachers in my school to whom I rarely paid enough attention.

MINDFULNESS AND MEDITATION

Jonathan Haidt's book, *The Happiness Hypothesis,* looks at the science of happiness and discusses a broad range of things that are thought to influence our happiness as humans. From the myriad list of things you might expect to be high on that list (like money, job satisfaction, certain houses or lifestyles, our football team winning regularly, sex, TV, buying new things, etc), when you review the scientific evidence, very few things actually have a lasting effect on happiness. But two big *negative* influences on happiness are:

1. Noise pollution: living or working somewhere very noisy is one of the few things the human brain struggles to make allowances for.

2.   A regular and long commute to work/college: commuting a long distance for study or work has been proven to make you less happy, no matter how much you tell yourself you'll fill the time with books or audiobooks or work or fun.

But things that will actually make you happier, and are scientifically proven to do so? One of the very few things for which overwhelming evidence exists to suggest a happiness boost is meditation. I live in Brighton, which is probably the UK's capital of meditation: in fact it's the UK capital of anything remotely 'woowoo', spiritual, hippy or self-developmental. So I've spent a few years surrounded by people for whom meditation and mindfulness techniques are not a new thing, but I can visit other parts of the UK or parts of the world where it's seen as mystical and a bit alien. So if meditation is a new concept to you and you've never tried it, let me reassure you, it's simple, it doesn't matter if you're religious or not, it's easy to get started with and it's generally a wonderful little well-kept secret.

If you're one of those people thinking, 'yeah, I've tried it, but it never sticks' or, 'I see the benefits but I don't know where to start', then that's my aim in this little section: to help you build it as a habit.

SO WHAT IS MEDITATION?

I once had a meditation teacher in India who I was asking about which techniques to learn, which books to buy and which courses to do. It was clear to her that I was trying to 'fix' my problem of not meditating regularly in the way us Westerners do best: we look to find something external to consume. She let me think through all the options and then she just smiled and said: 'Dude, just sit.'

And that was a light bulb moment for me. The answer wasn't in me buying more things or taking more courses. I just had to get better at sitting down and doing nothing. Because really, that's all meditation really takes.

THE ELEPHANT AND THE MONKEY

The effects of meditation on the brain are best explained by imagining a monkey riding on the back of an elephant. The monkey is your conscious mind, the elephant your subconscious mind. The elephant wants to be slow and measured and grounded, whereas the monkey wants to chatter, make mischief, move from one direction to the next and generally create havoc. The monkey is in a constant state of agitation, yet it is too small to control the elephant.

So the effect of meditation is to silence the monkey. Often this isn't possible, so you're just getting to a state where its chatter no longer affects your direction of travel. When you do this you're less impulsive, you're more grounded and you're better equipped to sit for long periods of study. And here's the real key: you remember we talked about how attention was our most precious resource and in particular our proactive attention? Well, by meditating regularly, you can actually increase this resource. No-one attempting time management can magically 'grow' more time, but anyone attempting attention management can increase their supply of proactive attention.

Here's the five-step guide to how to meditate:

1. Sit comfortably somewhere.

2. Try to focus on something specific, so that you become aware of your attention – most meditation teachers will suggest focussing on your own breathing, in and out, perhaps counting each breath, but you could also look at a picture or a candle, or focus on a sound of your choosing.

3. Notice when other thoughts arise. You'll notice I used the word 'notice', not 'feel guilty about' or 'try to get rid of'.

4. Keep focussing on your breathing or the candle or whatever else you decided to focus on.

5. Keep doing that some more, until it's time to stop.

And that's it. Even five minutes a day of doing this can make a huge difference. You can also do this as part of taking short breaks from your studies. And because it doesn't require any equipment or technology, you can do it on the bus, or even walking down the street.

Headspace and Buddhify

We practise meditation in the office of my company, Think Productive, every morning. We use a guided meditation app called 'Headspace' to do this, which has a neat little ten-day programme called 'Take 10'. It's ten minutes of meditation every day for ten days. Everything you need to succeed is right there: you can measure your progress and watch short video explanations to deepen your understanding.

Another great app is Buddhify. This one is all about 'meditation for busy people' (perfect when you're juggling learning and life!) and has some great suggestions and guided meditations for places like trains or inner-city spaces. Again, it's full of all the guidance you could possibly need to help make the habit stick.

If you are struggling to fit meditation into a busy lifestyle, then these apps can help.

EXERCISE: MEDITATION

Try a ten-minute meditation right now, using the five-step process above, or one of the apps. At the end of the ten minutes, try to reflect on what you found easy or difficult about it. You may find ten minutes an incredibly long time to think about nothing and do nothing (it's longer than it sounds at first!), but by developing the awareness of what's working and what's difficult, you'll begin to make the habit stick.

THE POMODORO TECHNIQUE

What has a kitchen timer got to do with productivity? Well, Francesco's Cirillo's book, *The Pomodoro Technique*, is all about using a kitchen timer to manage your attention, working in dashes that count down from 25 minutes to zero, followed by a five-minute break. The idea is that during each 'Pomodoro', you screen out procrastination and distractions, knowing that you have a five-minute break coming up. It's also a great motivator as you can see the timer ticking down, so you challenge yourself to get as much done during the 25 minutes as possible. Then, by stopping after 25 minutes, you are able to maintain a more balanced flow of energy throughout the day rather than reaching mid-afternoon and already feeling frazzled. This works because breaking after 25 minutes usually means interrupting yourself mid-flow, rather than waiting until your brain is feeling tired. It's a particularly great technique for people easily prone to distractions, or if you're trying to develop more Ninja Focus for one particular topic or activity (such as note-taking, exam revision or writing assignments), where it helps to break it down into smaller chunks of time. As the old saying goes, if you want to eat an elephant, the only way to do it is one mouthful at a time! You can find out more at pomodorotechnique.com, where Francesco has a whole bunch of resources to help you use his technique more effectively.

EXERCISE: POMODOROS

Think about a task you have coming up that's going to take an hour or more. Break the task down into 25-minute dashes (Pomodoros). How many Pomodoros do you think you'll need to complete the activity?

Use this to measure the activity as you go, too – it's a great way to develop your awareness of how long things take and of how you use your own time and attention.

One of the reasons people are put off using the Pomodoro Technique is that they think they'll have to use a loudly ticking kitchen timer – which isn't really sustainable if you're working in the library or on a kitchen table surrounded by your family! Luckily, help is  at hand, and there are many inexpensive or free apps that replicate the 25-minute countdown, just without all the noise. You can also get apps for your computer, such as www.mytomatoes.com, which sit in the corner of the screen – particularly helpful if you want to spend an hour or two without your smartphone but still want the playful focus of Pomodoro.

LECTURES AND CLASSES

One of the hardest places to pay attention is in lectures and classes. This isn't surprising, given that a study conducted by The National Training Laboratories in the USA found that students retain only about 5% of what they are taught in lectures. This is by far the lowest of any academic format (reading offers a 10% retention rate, discussion groups 50% and learning by doing 75%). So here are some tips and approaches to help you make the most of your lectures:

1. **Avoid 'first flight'.** Make the lecture your *last* exposure to the information, not your first. Most students make the mistake of arriving at the lecture ready for a voyage of discovery. Instead, treat the lectures as tools to confirm or 'glue together' your previous reading. Aim to have a good understanding of the topic *before* the lecture. And before you think that this creates extra

work, think about how much more time it takes to scrabble around two days before an assignment or test precisely because you're trying to recall what on earth that lecture was about! So why not invest the time up front instead, and avoid the stress? A Ninja recognizes the value of Preparedness.

2. **'How was it for you?'** After a lecture, try to ask at least two other people: 'What was the highlight there for you?' Take some time to gauge reactions to the lecture. If the lecture was really bad, you're in danger of worrying and struggling on your own unless you have this confirmed! And presuming it wasn't terrible, it's always a good idea to seek out some different perspectives. In doing so, you might find that it reconfirms the key learning for you, or helps you question your own thinking and develop new ideas.

3. **Take it home.** Take advantage of any other resources such as the PowerPoint slides or lecture recordings. Spending another hour with the material, recapping and refreshing your perspective further, can actually be done when you don't have high levels of attention – you can see it as a nice 'treat' at the end of a long day of studying to sit back and be a bit more passive with your learning.

4. **Change your view.** If you have a number of classes or lectures in the same room, try not to sit in the same part of the room each time. Humans are creatures of habit and we tend to repeat what we've done before, but by sitting in different parts of the room, we create a different way to remember each lecture. The more extreme you can be with this the better: front row, back row, left aisle, right aisle.

5. **Look for scaffolding.** Think about it from the tutor's point of view. In any class or lecture, they're trying to tell you a story.

Stories have beginnings, middles and ends. The beginning sets the scene, or perhaps picks up from or recaps from last time. It will introduce questions or 'jeopardy' – some kind of problem or question that will need to be solved. The middle part will be the main information. In stories, the middle part is usually where the hero or heroine is struggling against evil powers or trying to find their way home. In the same way, think about what the questions are, what the 'struggle' is, what the other 'characters' might be telling us. And the ending is about conclusion. Battles for ideas are won and lost. You might also want to think about what the personal 'battle' or 'satisfactory ending' is for your tutor: what is their viewpoint? What are they hoping to convince you of? What's the main gift they're trying to give you?

Of course, there are a host of other skills that come into play to make sure that you get the most out of each lecture or class. We'll move on to look at note-taking and reading in more detail later in this chapter (as well as complementary skills like memory techniques later in the book), but I hope what you see is a pattern emerging: paying attention and paying *quality* attention is a skill. It's something you can work on and improve.

TACKLING LONG AND BORING LECTURES AND CLASSES

Teachers and lecturers are more familiar with academic research about learning and attention spans than most, yet there are still many lecturers that insist on two- or even three-hour lectures without proper breaks, deliberately ignoring the difficulty this presents for students. If your teacher or lecturer really insists on long sessions, it's time for you to take matters into your own hands. Here are a few examples of things you can do quite easily:

1. **Take your own breaks.** Get outside and get fresh air. While you might miss a few minutes, you'll pay better attention to the rest of the session if you do.

2. **Move around the room.** If it's not too conspicuous, move from the front to the back of the room. Even doing this means stretching your legs and increasing blood flow to the brain.

3. **Snack.** A little blood sugar rush helps.

4. **Tag-team it.** This is an extreme idea for particularly incompetent or boring lecturers. Team up with a friend and work the lectures in shifts! Instead of a three-hour lecture, you do an hour and a half, taking great notes. Then the other half of the lecture, you rely on your friends' notes. Doing this and knowing that your friend is relying on the notes you take (and vice versa) is a massive incentive.

5. **Tear it out and tear it up.** The next page is for you to tear out and use. You can decide if you deliver it by hand with a smile, or adopt more of a Stealth and Camouflage style …

READING

Reading is an English town not far from Oxford. Sorry, terrible joke. But a terrible joke that does have a purpose. It illustrates that there's reading and there's reading. There's reading passively without really questioning meaning or context and then there's reading actively and critically, focussing not just on the subject matter and the words, but questioning why those words were chosen and what the person writing them was influenced by.

CRITICAL READING

It's important to read analytically and critically, not simply to go through the words in your head. I like to think the best way to do this is to start an imaginary conversation with the author. Everything you read has been written by another human being, each with their own perspectives, baggage and biases. Sometimes, depending on

YOU'VE BEEN NINJA'D!

Dear Lecturer,

You've been Ninja'd. It has been brought to my attention as Chief Ninja that some of my trainee Study Ninjas are losing focus in your sessions. I am writing to ask you to consider the following ideas to make your students' learning more engaging. I am sure that by implementing some of the ideas here, you'll dramatically improve their happiness – and they'll learn better too.

- Please keep talks to a maximum of 50 minutes, followed by discussion or Q&A. Any longer than this and they would really appreciate the opportunity to go for a wee and have a break.

- Make it as interactive as possible.

- Please help the Visual learners by including lots of nice diagrams and preferably plenty of pictures of cats and bunnies. You could also learn to juggle or wear Noel Edmonds-style jumpers for comic visual effect.

- Please use multimedia (I know, your tech department is a pain, but it really helps).

- And we'd love it if you did a funny every once in a while too.

Thank you for your co-operation. And congratulations, you've just made a Study Ninja very happy.

what you're reading, you'll need to take into account how the author pays their bills. For example, is that maverick opinion piece about government health provision being written by someone who regularly receives payment from a private health company? What's their agenda? What could be behind their writing? Or is it a peer-reviewed journal article, based not on opinions but on thorough academic findings? This will of course give the article more credence if you cite it in an assignment, but depending on your course and subject matter, you might be looking to read a broader range of material to get a wider understanding of a topic (particularly true of arts and humanities subjects).

THEORY VS FACTS

What evidence do you see for the arguments presented? Are you really reading someone's theory or opinions, or are you reading facts? Does the author back up what is written, proving it from credible sources? Basing conclusions on opinions or blind faith, however passionately written, is different from working from facts.

While this may sound like an obvious distinction in the world of academia, think about this from the point of view of the rest of your life. So much of what we read these days is mere opinion, and as a society we are often being led by the majority's view, rather than actually looking at the facts. The media, too, plays a huge role in this. Again, think about who pays the journalists at our newspapers or on the TV news – never confuse a biased opinion with fact, just because it sounds official and is delivered by someone wearing a suit!

RUDYARD KIPLING'S SIX HONEST SERVING MEN

Developing the ability to think critically about any text is exactly that – a skill. The same is true for critical thinking in life in general. When I need to evaluate something quickly, I often turn to a poem by Rudyard Kipling and use this as a guide through my exploration of the topic in question. Kipling's poem is simple to remember and goes like this:

> I keep six honest serving men,
> (They taught me all I knew);
> Their names are What and Why and When,
> And How and Where and Who
> —Rudyard Kipling (from *Just So Stories*, 1902)

These 'six honest serving men' have served me well over the years, too. Asking good questions is the key to critical thinking. Here are a few simple examples of the six honest serving men in action:

What

▶ What is the person writing this trying to achieve?

▶ What is their motivation?

Why

▶ Why are they making that particular argument?

▶ Why is this important to us, or to others?

When

▶ When was this written? Is it the latest research in this area?

▶ When might this theory not be true?

How

▶ How was this work done?

▶ How else might this be proved? How might we disprove this?

Where

▶ Where could this work lead us to? (What's next in this field?)

▶ Where is the person coming from?

Who

▶ Who is the person writing this? (What's their role/job/background?)

▶ Who else benefits from this conclusion? (And is there a connection?)

▶ Who else is interested in this?

The six honest serving men are like a little checklist I carry around with me in my head. It's useful in so many different contexts. If I'm planning an event for example, making sure the marketing includes sufficient details that answer the basic questions of what, why, when, how, where and who is a great way to know I have all the bases covered. If I'm worried about a particular problem I need to solve, these questions help me to think about things from different angles. So developing critical reading skills is really about developing critical thinking skills. And what this means is you can do this almost anywhere, with almost any subject matter.

PAID-FOR OPINIONS AND THE QUEST TO TELL STORIES

My English teacher at school, Paddy Wex, had a poster on his wall that talked about the characteristics of British newspapers, designed to make you think about the people behind the headlines. Here's my recollection from memory:

'*The Times* is read by the people who run the country.

The *Guardian* is read by the people who think they ought to run the country.

The *Daily Mail* is read by the wives of the people who run the country.

The *Financial Times* is read by the people who own the country.

The *Morning Star* is read by the people who think the country ought to be run by another country.

The *Daily Telegraph* is read by people who think it already is.

And the *Sun* is read by people who don't care who runs the country, as long as she's sexy.'

Along with the six honest serving men, I try to bear this in mind whenever I'm reading or watching anything – like TV news – that might be full of hidden agendas.

EXERCISE: CRITICAL READING

Pick five different newspapers and look at them on their front pages on the same day (you can of course do this online by going to their homepages and having five windows open on your screen, but either buying the newspapers or standing in the shop for a few minutes and looking at them all works better). Think about the following questions:

1. Which story is their front-page headline? Why have they chosen that one?

2. What else is on their front page, and why?

3. Pick a controversial story of the day and read how each of the newspapers is covering the story – what are the differences in tone you notice? What pieces of information are higher up the story in some newspapers, but barely mentioned in others? (Journalists usually write with the assumption that most people give up reading somewhere between the beginning and the end, so tend to put their most important stuff nearer the beginning).

4. Think about …

   - the owners of the newspaper – who are their friends and enemies?

   - the typical reader of the newspaper (think about who you know who might read each paper)

   - your own biases before you read the articles. What made you agree or disagree most vigorously?

5. If you're doing all of this while standing in the newsagents' shop, leave now before the server makes you buy all those newspapers!

Reading critically starts with thinking critically. I am a strong believer that we should continually test our own assumptions and look for the shades of grey, rather than treat everything as black and white. It's important to ask questions and explore issues from wildly sceptical, optimistic and realistic view points. To do so means looking beyond the information that's presented to you and exploring where it comes from, its meanings and motivations. This is something that you can practise in day-to-day life. Doing so means that when it comes to reading critically, or thinking critically as part of your study, you'll have your skills well-honed. Let's look at critical thinking in the day-to-day.

EXERCISE: CRITICAL THINKING

This is something you can do almost anywhere. Whether you're watching TV, travelling on a bus, talking to friends or walking down the street.

Pick a subject matter. It could be the TV show, the bus, what you see out of the window, your friends or simply the T-shirt your friend is wearing. Go through each of the six honest serving men in turn and ask at least two questions about the subject matter you've chosen. So if you're on the bus, you might ask:

Why … does this bus route cover these particular areas?

Who … runs the bus?

Who else … cares that the bus service works well?

Or if you're looking at a friend's T-shirt with a slogan you might ask:

What … is your friend trying to say?

Why … is this important to them?

How … might this affect others or yourself?

Practise asking questions, however small or banal the topic appears to be. Each time you do this, you're developing your critical thinking skills. A sense of healthy scepticism and childlike curiosity will ultimately enhance your learning, as well as make it way more interesting than just trying to memorize facts.

READING AS A SKILL

Reading is also a very time-consuming activity, particularly if handled badly. So in this section, we'll look at reading as a skill, reading lists and reading with Ninja-efficiency. There are different types of reading. What a Ninja knows for sure is that there simply isn't time to read everything thoroughly or perfectly. Different styles of reading take up different amounts of time and attention. It's important to practise Ninja Ruthlessness here – to be totally focussed on the final outcome we're trying to achieve, and tailor our reading accordingly. Just like the internet, books occupy the paradox of being both your best friend and your worst enemy, depending on how you use them. The difference between trying to read the right things and trying to read *everything* is the difference between success and failure.

My reading habits have certainly become more ruthless with each passing year. The ultimate example of this is watching me read a paper magazine. I am subscribed to a couple of professional journals that maybe contain nine or ten lengthy pieces, all of which would have some level of interest to my work. Yet I'll start by skimming through the whole journal in no more than five minutes. From there, I'll pick out perhaps four articles to spend more time on, which I'll then either tear out of the journal, throwing the rest straight into the recycling, or I'll speed-read a little more before narrowing down to just one or two. Might I miss really good or useful stuff with that approach? Yes, of course. But knowing that in doing so, I am going to spend the time ingesting and digesting the one or two articles that will *really* take me somewhere amazing depends on me ruthlessly tossing out the rest. Again, did you see what happened there? Ruthlessness and the rule of 80-20!

Instapaper

I'm less disciplined when it comes to internet reading, but I'm working on it. Most people find avoiding getting distracted by reading harder when it comes to the internet than they do with physical reading, mainly because headline writers and site design-ers are constantly using analytics and feedback to learn everything they can about your attention habits to keep you 'hooked' on their sites. And of course information is available more seamlessly than with books or magazines, so it's easier to keep exploring, either unaware of or blissfully ignoring what you're supposed to be doing. To deal with this, I use an app called Instapaper, which is on my iPad. Then, on my web browser, I have an extension for Instapaper, which bookmarks the articles that I want to read and then sends them to my iPad's app. So it means that I can get halfway through something that looks useful, realize I'm getting distracted from whatever else I was supposed to be doing and then have a way to save that reading for later. Without that app (or something similar) in place, it's so easy to think, 'if I don't read this now, I'll lose it forever' or, 'I'll forget to come back to it', so having a system set up to store reading material helps to solve the problem. Also, it serves to make it a more pleasurable experience because I end up reading it on a tablet screen on my sofa, rather than sitting at my desk reading from a computer screen.

Once we're clear on the impact we're looking for from our reading, there are three main styles of reading, starting from the fastest (and most Ruthless) through to the slowest (and most enjoyable!):

1. Mining

2. Speed-reading

3. Feast-reading

MINING

Mining isn't really reading at all, it's cheating. But cheating (ethically, of course) is a vital skill to develop in so many areas of life, including reading. Mining is about looking only for particular information. It's a particularly useful skill to develop if you're researching for assignments and want to show a breadth of information or sources. Mining is the equivalent of how I go shopping: I walk into the shop with a specific intention in mind of what I'm hoping to buy, heading single-mindedly to the area of the shop that should help me, then I either find what I want or don't – but either way I'm in and out of the shop at top speed. Here are a few things that mining can be particularly handy for:

► finding books or articles that support a particular argument (articles with executive summaries are a joy when mining and the summary becomes the *only* bit a miner reads)

► finding specific facts

► finding quotes, or nice bits of 'added value' information

► eliminating half the reading list

HOW TO MINE

Mining a whole page of text in a book or on a screen should take no more than a few seconds. Hence, mining isn't really reading at all; it's the quickest and most selective form of scanning there is. To do this, you first need to think of what words you're looking for. I find it helps for me to visualize the shape of that word in my head before I start running my eyes down the page. Doing this allows me to home in on those words (or move on) with maximum speed.

CHOOSE YOUR WEAPONS CAREFULLY

The words you choose to look for when mining make a huge differ-ence to how useful a process it will be. It may also be helpful to think of mining as a technique to help you familiarize yourself with a text before you're going to start reading it in more detail. Here are some of the best kinds of words to choose when you start mining:

▶ **Scrabble-factor words.** Longer words, and those with the least commonly used consonants (such as K, X, Y and Z) are easier to find quickly.

▶ **Names and numbers.** Capital letters in names help them stand out, numbers – such as dates or page numbers – do the same.

▶ **Rare words.** If you're still not sure where to begin, go for words that are likely to be less common in the next.

Ctrl+F

A Weapon-savvy Study Ninja will have already spent some time honing their keyboard shortcut skills. But if you aren't using 'Ctrl+F' regularly, you need to be. On any website, use Ctrl+F to pull up a search bar in your browser. Use this to search for the words you want to find. This is particularly useful for looking for facts or references to particular people or studies, but it's also a great way to see a large document on the web in a new way – a super-quick scan through the document, looking for the highlighted words, can help you to see patterns and even the narrative flow of a piece of writing, rather than just staring at a screen full of text. You can also use Ctrl+F in Word documents, PDFs and other formats.

BOOK BLITZING

You can also think of mining as a way of whittling down many books – particularly if you have a long reading list to contend with. As soon as you get the reading list, head straight to the library and invest an hour in finding every single book on the reading list and making short notes about each, spending no more than two minutes on each book. Make notes about how accessible the book feels. Is it long? Does it look fun and easy to read? Does it feel very close to your interests or further away? First impressions count.

SPEED-READING

Speed-reading, or 'skimming', is the process of reading and understanding the text as quickly as possible. In the 1960s and 1970s it became a common and popular practice, buoyed by American Presidents John F. Kennedy and Jimmy Carter being renowned practitioners and advocates (President Carter was pictured taking speed-reading classes in the White House with his daughter, and both Presidents encouraged their staff to take such training too). You may have also seen advertisements online or even posted near to your school or campus that invite you to learn 'miraculous' techniques that will enable you to learn whole subjects in fifteen minutes, though the bad news is that if a particular programme is claiming something that sounds too good to be true, it probably is.

Let's look at the facts when it comes to speed-reading. Speed-reading is not the same as 'feast-reading' (most people's normal pace for standard reading, which we'll cover shortly). It's possible to read faster, but of course the trade-off is less comprehension. The faster you read, the more you might miss. However, notice the word 'might' there! Again, the 80-20 rule is at play here, and it's often possible to understand enough of the text by reading much more quickly. Again, this kind of selective Ruthlessness allows you to read a much broader breadth of material than just reading normally. A typical 'normal' pace of reading is between 200 and 300 words per minute, whereas those who practise speed-reading regularly can read at anywhere from around 600 to even up to 1000 words per minute. So while it's far from a magic silver bullet that will change your life, it's still a great weapon to have at your disposal, to allow you to be selective and get to the 'gist' of something as quickly as possible.

HOW DO I LEARN TO SPEED-READ?

Speed-reading is actually a set of three or four key habits, and improving them is as much about recognizing and breaking current bad habits as it is about starting brand new ones. Here are the things that you really need to stop doing if you want to develop as a speed-reader:

1. Don't read word by word

The way we're taught to read is to focus on each word at a time. If you're fully 'in flow' with your reading, you might find that your eyes are glancing a few words ahead, but we tend to go at a pace that feels comfortable and move our eyes more slowly than we have the potential to. Try reading the next sentence with your eyes moving at twice the speed and you'll see what I mean.

2. Avoid 'sub-vocalization'

Sub-vocalization is when you're reading the words 'out loud' in your own head, and listening for your own voice reading the words back to you in order to obtain the meaning of the words. This is something we're taught to do from a very early age, so it's a tricky thing to try and undo. But the first step is to realize that it's what you're doing. You hear that little version of you in your brain? The one frantically trying to read the words out loud but also panicked because I told you to read it all at double speed? Yes, that's the one. Stop doing that! Because reading the words aloud in your head means you're always limited in terms of how fast you can read, based on the speed you can 'talk'.

3. Avoid recapping

What you may also have noticed if you're trying to read more quickly is that the brain keeps saying things like: 'Wait a second. What did that word mean? Did it say Harold or Herod?' So as you try to increase the pace of your reading, you also have to ruthlessly avoid skipping back and recapping bits of the text. This slows you down.

Now let's look at what you can work on in order to turn those three habits into positive speed-reading assets:

1. Read in chunks

Instead of word-by-word reading, read either in lines, or in chunks of a few words at a time. Your job is to see each word, but not necessarily to read each word. The brain has a marvellous ability to join the dots, filling in the blanks you left behind and leaving you with a pretty decent comprehension of what the text is about. To help with this, you can use a ruler, a pen or the large font or zoom setting on your e-reader or tablet to keep things moving quickly.

2. Let the words flow over you and increase your speed

Don't try to read aloud in your head. Focus instead on the visual patterns of the words. Focus on the speed and momentum of your eyes. The eyes are capable of moving faster and viewing a wider area than just word by word, but if you're finding the speed difficult to achieve, it often helps here to soften your gaze, or hold the text slightly further away from you. Move the pen or ruler across the page to keep the momentum, or click from page to page if you're viewing something digitally. The trick here is to start gauging your comfort and success by the speed rather than by the comprehension of every word – and as you get comfortable with a faster speed, make yourself slightly uncomfortable again with an even faster speed!

3. Never go back – think 'anti-perfection'

Remember that your job here is not to understand every word of what you're reading. Your job here is to get the general gist of the piece. So don't be tempted to turn back. Keep moving that pointer, keep the momentum and become supremely relaxed in the knowledge that you're not aiming for perfection. In fact, proactively seeking 'anti-perfection' is what I've found to be the best way around this. Knowing that you're missing things – which is not what we're taught to do at school! – can feel a bit stressful or wrong. But what you're developing here is a new way of reading. It isn't one you're going to use for everything, but it will complement and aid the other forms of reading that you do.

4. Practise in a quiet place

As you're developing this skill, you should be constantly challenging yourself to go that little bit faster. What this means is you're asking your brain to fill in more of the gaps, at increasingly demanding speeds. So don't give your brain lots of other things to do at the same time! Find a quiet place to speed-read, where you're free from distractions and able to truly Focus.

5. Measure your progress

You might also like to time yourself every once in a while to see if your practice is paying off. You might be surprised how a little attention paid to a skill that we generally take for granted can actually make a huge difference to how you approach your learning. Keep a note of how long it takes to read a standard page of A4 text. Cut and paste text into Word documents or even into a speed-reading app in order to get an accurate and like-for-like comparison.

Spreeder.com

Spreeder.com is a neat web app that allows you to practise your speed-reading. You simply cut and paste text from any article or website into the square in the middle of the screen, and then allow the app to display the  words back to you on the screen either as single words or in chunks, at whatever speed of words per minute you choose. It's a great tool for measuring your current reading speed, and then something you can come back to both for practice and also to measure your progress over time.

Readingsoft.com

Readingsoft is a free online speed-reading test. It presents you with a piece of text and you use start and stop buttons to time yourself reading it. It's a great way to gauge your current level, reading text in a more normal format than Spreeder offers, so my advice would be to practise on Spreeder and then measure on Readingsoft.com

EXERCISE: SPEED TRAINING

If you have never tried speed-reading before, find a piece of text either from an online journal, or from an article you want to read. Cut and paste the text into the big box on Spreeder.com and adjust the settings to read the piece at different speeds. Try to get into that state where you are no longer reading each word and hearing the reading voice in your head. Play with the settings, experiment and test yourself. If you have time, you may also want to test your speed using Readingsoft.com, and then repeat the experiment next week to see if you can improve your 'words per minute' count.

FEAST-READING

Feast-reading is what you reserve for only the most important articles and books. Feasting on something that's truly electrifying to read is one of life's greatest pleasures. Unfortunately, when reading is so associated with hard work and the drudgery of day-to-day study, it can be easy to overlook this. So we need to reclaim reading as a simple pleasure. And to do this, we need a clear line between all that drudgery (i.e. mining and speed-reading) and the good stuff. What you've done with those two, faster styles of reading is use the 80-20 rule to increase efficiency. Feast-reading is, in my opinion, just as efficient as speed-reading – but only as long as you're sure that what you're reading is one of the most influential or useful things you could read to aid your learning. We don't have time to put our fullest attention onto everything, but there are times when only your fullest attention will do.

HOW SHOULD I FEAST-READ?

Feast-reading doesn't involve any special techniques. You can 'sub-vocalize' if you like. Get lost in the text. Make notes. Have fun with your imagination. Of course, there are a few good practices that most of us ignore in day-to-day life that can aid your level of comprehension and memory when it comes to feast-reading:

NINJA STEALTH AND CAMOUFLAGE

To truly get lost in a great book, you should be somewhere no-one can find you!

WEAPON-SAVVY

Work out your preferred medium for reading. What makes reading easier and more pleasurable for you? Do you prefer a digital reader or a book? Do you prefer a Kindle with the white background, or the shiny screen? Do you prefer large-print A4 or smaller text? Of course if you're borrowing books from the library it's not always possible to dictate this, but rather than adopting a piecemeal approach, think about this question now and complete the sentence:

'If I could choose my favourite way to read everything, I'd choose ...'

MINDFULNESS

When reading, it's worth thinking about distractions as both an external and internal thing. There's a reason we started early on in this book with getting organized. It's because it helps you feel in control. And when you feel in control, you nag yourself less and get fewer distractions whirring round in your mind. So before you sit down to read, scribble down any new to-do list items onto a piece of paper or into your phone. Get all of that 'gunk' out of your head so that your mind is clear and ready for Ninja Focus. It might also help to do a quick five-minute meditation, too.

BREAK REGULARLY TO INCREASE YOUR MEMORY

Psychologists call this the 'primacy and recency effect'. What this means is that your brain is more likely to remember the bits from the beginning and end of a session of reading. So if you take small but regular breaks, you'll have more beginnings and more ends than if you sit for hours at a time, or take fewer but longer breaks.

Use feast-reading to excite you again. Use feast-reading to convince the Lazy, Scatterbrained version of you, who has just spent a week bumming around with friends and learning next to nothing, that an hour sat by a fireplace studiously feast-reading will make you look 'all academic'. Because it will. But that hour of indulgence may also have a less superficial purpose too: it may fire you up to get your Ninja mojo back. It might remind you why you chose to study this subject in the first place.

READING LISTS

The best thing about books is that they can take you anywhere. The worst thing about books is that they can take you anywhere.

A course reading list is a prime inducer of Distant Deadline Deficiency – getting through it feels like a daunting task, and one that you can easily put off until tomorrow. We may start flirting with it in week one of term, even take out a few books in a fit of enthusiasm, but it's fair to say that reading lists are not properly used very often.

SAVING TIME WITH READING: CHOOSING WISELY

We've talked a lot in this section about the rule of 80-20 and its importance to reading and learning. One of the things that gets in the way of people reading efficiently is perfectionism and guilt. I think this comes from our early school days. We're told to get all our spelling right, get ten out of ten in our tests, clear our plates, do up our shoelaces, tidy our rooms. None of these things are inherently bad, but what they build up in our minds is a strong narrative of perfectionism and conformity, and the idea that to succeed we must get everything absolutely right, and what's more, in exactly the same way as everybody else.

Many people assume they should try to tackle reading lists in the same way they tackled their school spelling tests, aiming to read every book on the list from beginning to end. So here's the two words I want you to memorize, recite and live by. The secret source of being a Study Ninja?

'Just enough'

This is your aim. Just enough. Not all, not most and not what you see everyone else doing. Just enough. Doing just enough when you were younger was considered lazy or naughty. Now, it's the only way to stay sane. And trust me, it's no different in workplace productivity:

when you're getting 600 emails a day and your days are booked out with back-to-back meetings, that childhood narrative of perfection and conformity can be one of the most stress-inducing and damaging ways you can possibly think. So look at your reading list like a restaurant menu. You might focus on a few key dishes, or you might try a sample menu where you try small portions of lots of things on offer, but trying to get through everything on the menu would just leave you feeling sick.

EXERCISE: READING REFLECTION

Spend a few minutes reflecting on how you read. After all, it's probably the activity that takes up the most time and attention! Think about …

▶ which reading styles here am I most or least comfortable with, and why?

▶ what could I change or experiment with here?

Before you finish, make a brief plan for your next pieces of reading.

NOTE-TAKING

New term, new notebook. We all know that feeling. And we've also all looked back to the first pages of a notebook and sensed that early-days-of-term optimism in our handwriting, or the good habits that are present on those first pages, only to see them fade away. But beyond your base levels of enthusiasm, there's a science to note-taking that can seriously help or hinder you as you look to capture your learning and cement it. There are lots of styles of note-taking, some that you might have already heard of and used, and some that you probably haven't.

HIGHLIGHTER PENS SUCK

One of the most common tools in learning is the good old-fashioned highlighter pen. However, did you know that there's little evidence to suggest that highlighting words in your notes or in books actually makes any difference to your memory? And there is also research that suggests that highlighting might 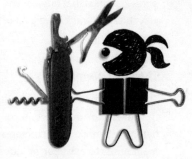 actually be a bad practice, because it hampers your ability to make connections between different facts or ideas. Far better to try writing things backwards or changing your writing style, which are more active processes than passively highlighting words.

The same is true of the standard practice of re-reading your notes. It's commonly done, but a lot of the research suggests that simply recapping, underlining and even rewriting notes may be next to useless. So it's worth developing some habits and techniques that will force you to think a little harder, ask yourself questions and interact with your notes in a different way, rather than just settling for different versions of passively re-reading things.

THE CORNELL SYSTEM

The Cornell System is a way of note-taking developed by Walter Pauk, a professor at Cornell University. It helps to prompt questions and create a 'dialogue' with your notes, rather than just creating notes to be re-read and highlighted. The idea is to divide the page into three sections, as pictured here:

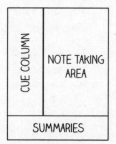

The Note-taking column

The main part of the page is where you take 'normal' notes. You're recording key words, phrases, things that interest you, and if you're paying attention all the way through, you'll have a bit of a narrative structure of the 'story' the tutor is telling.

The Cue Column

The idea of the cue column is that after the lecture, you might revisit the notes and add in certain 'cues' – the key words or phrases that will help you to make the learning stick in your mind. You might use the main notes to ask yourself questions during the class, but then use the cue column afterwards to try to answer those questions. You can also use the cue section to perhaps predict likely exam questions.

The Summary Section

The idea of the summary section is that you'll revisit the notes within 24 hours and make a summary of them.

MIND MAPS

Mind-mapping is a technique developed by Tony Buzan and widely used since the 1970s. Mind-mapping is a particularly useful way to take notes if you are a visual learner and can also be a great technique to help develop your thinking about the structures of information.

The basic structure of a mind map is as follows:

▶ The topic heading or idea is in the centre of the page.

▶ The topic's main themes then branch off and circle around the central topic, each described as either a key word or a drawing

▶ Smaller ideas or bits of information are 'twigs' that come off each of these branches, so as you move from the centre of the page to the outside, the information goes from biggest to smallest, most central to most peripheral.

▶ Everything is connected back to the main topic, and you can see the connections 'mapped out'.

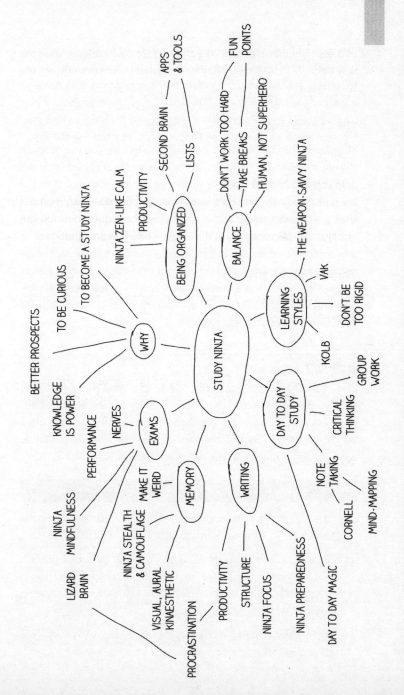

Personally, I find mind-mapping is a useful way to get an overview on a topic. If I'm learning something new, I will often use a mind map to reflect on what I've just learned, as a way of going back through my experience. And equally, if I'm feeling overwhelmed about a particular project or problem, then sitting quietly creating a mind map is one of the most reliable ways I know to reduce my stress about it.

ALTERNATIVES TO MIND-MAPPING

Mind-mapping is a very particular style of note-taking, which starts from a subject's 'middle' and then works quite chaotically from the inside out. I personally find it a really good way to group bits of information together and see the connections and patterns, but it's not for everyone. Others prefer grouping the information in tables, for example, or seeing a more linear flow with a clear start and finish using flow charts. The point here is to try things out and settle for what feels comfortable and effective.

USING NOTE-TAKING KEYS

One of the hardest things in the middle of a class is being able to write your notes as quickly as possible so that you can get your attention back fully to listening. Shorthand abbreviations and keys are a very useful part of this. You can make up your own of course, but here are a few suggestions that you can practise using:

Key	Means …
=	equals
E.g.	for example
<	less than
>	greater than
W/	with
W/o	without

Key	Means …
∴	therefore
Yr	year
→	So/leading to
*	Action (something for me to do)
⊗?	Likely exam question
Ref	reference
Re:	Regarding (about)
B/c	because
?	Question to think about

We'll be looking more at tips to commit your notes to memory in chapter seven.

Evernote

There are plenty of note-making apps for your computer, tablet and smartphone. By far the biggest and most popular of these is Evernote. Evernote is like a digital filing cabinet, or your digital 'bottom drawer'. It works by creating notes and notebooks to which you can add  tags, text, pictures and so on. The tablet app is easy to use, so you could even replace paper and input lecture or classroom notes directly into the app (although I'd recommend becoming an accomplished user first, as there's nothing less Weapon-savvy than being distracted by the tools when you're trying to do something important!)

There's loads of cool things you can do with it. I personally love to do paper-based mind maps and then take a photo of that with my phone, which I then add straight into Evernote (top tip – take photos of the sections but label the note with the name of the book, so that you have the reference handy when you need it later!). Evernote will even recognize and read the printed text from photos, so that you can then search for specific words – great if you want to quickly capture a specific section of a book without taking it out from the library. You can also of course do the same for web clippings, and there's also a function for you to email notes directly into Evernote.

Evernote is a free tool, but of course there's a premium version that you have to pay for. What's interesting about Evernote is that they have an unusually high rate of conversion from the free version to the paid subscription, which shows you that it's a product that lots of people really love. The free one will give you most of the good stuff, though. Finally, if your world is centred around Microsoft Office, the notes section of Outlook or Microsoft OneNote are great places to try too as alternatives. And if your world is more Google-centred then Google Keep would be worth a look too.

GoConqr

The other alternative to Evernote is GoConqr. This is a really cool web-based note-taking app that allows you to create mind maps, flashcards, quizzes and plain notes. It also allows you to make your own revision study timetable, access practice papers, and there's  also a social sharing side to it, so you can collaborate with course mates to share resources with each other. The downside is that at the time of writing, the tablet app lacks functionality, so if you wanted to use it to make notes during a class then it's not a good option without a reliable internet connection, but there are plenty of features that make this worth a look, particularly if you can get a group of course mates using it too and share your notes.

OH NO, IT'S GROUP WORK TIME!

It would be wrong in a book like this not to give some attention to group work. Group projects can be either the most exhilarating moments of learning or utter drudgery. Which category they fall into is mainly dependent on the motivations and personalities of the other people you're put in a group with – or stuck in a group with, if that's your point of view!

At its best, group work is a powerful learning tool, due to something called 'the generation effect'. Cognitive psychology studies have shown that people remember things better when they participated in them, rather than when they just passively read about them. I saw this first hand as a teacher in Uganda, lacking any science resources, and having to teach many of the things that I'd learned myself as a student through conducting active experiments. Hearing a story about a physics experiment is actually quite dull, no matter how hard you try. But seeing it or creating it yourself brings the whole thing to life very quickly.

There are two main problems with group work. Knowing these and being able to spot them in your group will help you make dull group work situations into magical learning experiences:

1. Group-think

'Group-think' is when operating in a group distorts your sense of reality. If you have a group of five people and two of them are wrong about something, you only need a doubt in the mind of one other person and suddenly you risk creating a majority of people who are wrong. And since no-one likes feeling left out, the group dynamic and longing to fit in is often enough to discourage critical thinking and persuade the other two people to support the majority view.

The same thing happens in matters of taste or judgement, because people don't like to be rude. So in a group, you'll convince yourselves that you've done a great job together, because you don't want to offend any of the individuals or create ripples of disharmony. Thus, five people on their own thinking critically about an issue and then coming together as a group to share their findings will usually lead you to a more constructive (but less polite) conclusion than everyone sat in a circle trying to be nice to each other.

Group-think is particularly prevalent when dealing with extreme high or low emotions. So groups will hype up any small victories and have the members of the group thinking they've just changed the world, whereas groups in a crisis will often convince themselves that their whole world is doomed.

HOW TO AVOID 'GROUP-THINK'

▶ **Seek first to understand, then to be liked.** No-one wants to put themselves in the position of being the odd one out in the group, but begin with the mindset that your first job is to learn and to contribute to the group, not to make the group like you. Recognizing that in life not everyone is going to like you is extremely liberating, once you get over the heartbreak of it all.

▶ **Think critically.** Are we really doing as well as we think? What are we missing? How would someone outside of this group perceive our current position?

▶ **Pose questions, not opposition.** To help your group avoid the group-think trap, you will need to pose some form of opposition to the prevailing wisdom of the group. Rather than stating your opposition directly, you can use questions as a way to see if you can tempt people over to your point of view. So rather than saying, 'I think we're getting a bit carried away here', you could ask: 'What else do we need to be thinking about?' That way, if your questions start to have any traction at all, you're seen as the constructive facilitator of success, not a destructive or negative force. Ninja stealth!

What you want to say	Instead, ask a question like …
'We're stuck on this one thing, and need to move on.'	'How are we for time?' 'What else do we need to be thinking about?'
'This approach is unrealistic.'	'What do we think the barriers/sticking points/difficulties might be with this approach?'
'This opinion is wrong.'	'What's our evidence to support this?'
'We're trying to do too much here.'	'Can we think about how long each bit of this will take?' 'Can we allocate some roles and responsibilities, so we can be clear on who's doing which bits?'

2. Social loafing

It's often said 'many hands make light work', implying that working in a group is more efficient than working alone. In fact, studies have found that the opposite is actually true. This is what psychologists refer to as 'social loafing'. Social loafing basically means putting in less effort because you know you're part of a group. Of course, there are occasions when the group will motivate you and you want to impress them, but in general, the Lazy, Scatterbrained version of you is much more likely to come to the fore in a group setting.

I remember one particular example of this from my university degree, where we had to present our findings on a large display board to be hung in the corridor of our department. We were asked to write our names at the bottom of the board so that the markers knew whose project was whose. There were six of us in the group, but one of the group members had been taking social loafing to a whole new level. He relied on the rest of us to do all the work, never attended our group meetings and didn't even contribute the one thing we'd delegated him to do in his absence. We were, however, required to add the names of all the group members, even if we felt aggrieved at their lack of effort. Cheekily, we wrote all our names in 16 point type at the bottom of the board, and then wrote his name in 6 point type. It was clear even without explanation the implication of this, and some of our lecturers had a good laugh about our 'statement'. The bad news in this story is that the next time I saw that guy (who was an extremely friendly but very lazy guy in general) he was on TV as a poker million-aire, proving that there really is no justice in the world.

HOW TO AVOID SOCIAL LOAFING:

Social loafing is inevitable, so you can't really avoid it, at least not in others. But here are a couple of useful tips that can help:

▶ **Allocate clear roles.** Don't leave anyone in the group without a role, from the very beginning.

▶ **Every action needs ONE owner.** Split as much of the 'work' of the group as you can into individual contributions, delegat-ing actions to single owners. Even things that are going to be done by two people should have one single 'owner' whose job is to be responsible to the rest of the group for making sure it's completed.

▶ **Review regularly.** Hold short, regular review meetings all the way through your group project. Even if your group work is just an hour's lesson, be the person who asks everyone to 'check in' and focus again on the task rather than getting carried away. If your group project lasts several weeks, suggest at least a weekly meet-ing. The more frequent the meetings, the more chance you have of being agile, changing the roles, rethinking and re-energising.

PRESENTATIONS

There's only one thing that's worse than group work – and that's group sessions where everybody's looking at you! Presentations can be nerve-inducing ordeals, but with a bit of Ninja Preparedness, you've got this covered. I've spent the last few years giving presentations all over the world. I've designed them, I've learned how to make content feel fresh even if I've delivered it a hundred times, and many, many times I've been stood in front of an audience, delivering something for the first time, feeling not quite sure what slides are coming after the ones I can see (or 'winging it', as it's sometimes called).

It's tragic how unengaging some presentations are, especially when you know that if you stripped away those nerves, there's an engaging presenter in there somewhere, bursting to get out and make a big impact. So here are my golden rules for presentations.

1. **Don't hide behind your slides.** If you ignore all the rest of the advice, please follow this one. Nothing ruins a presentation quite like this. We've all seen it. There are seven bullet points on each slide, and you're sat in a room, reading the slides, while someone stands at the front reading it along with you. They're  not adding anything, or talking around the slides. They're reading – hiding – and can't wait until it's time to sit down again.

2. **The ten word rule.** Here's a great way to avoid the above. You should never have seven bullet points on a slide. In fact, my rule is no more than ten words on a slide. That's it. If it's longer than that, it should be another slide. Importantly, this rule does two things: it focusses you on the visual side of a slide (great slides engage the audience with pictures) and secondly, it forces you to think about what you're going to actually say, as opposed to thinking just about what's going on the slide.

3. If you need to convey more detailed information, **do this via a printed handout**. People love a handout. If nothing else it

allows them to occasionally drift off, knowing they won't miss anything. They also appreciate the effort. So put wordy text on handouts, not on slides.

4. **Make your slides pretty, not whizzy.** Keep the pictures attractive and engaging, but keep the animations and transitions as simple as possible. If you've ever seen someone present with 'Prezi', you'll know what I mean (if you haven't, basically I despise Prezi).

5. **Ask the audience.** Ask questions, get them involved and engage with them. Very few speakers are interesting enough on their own to hold a whole room's attention for fifteen minutes, let alone an hour. So break it up, create dialogue and offer them opportunities to participate.

6. **Use 'presenter view' or cue cards.** Personally, I set up my laptop as a PowerPoint monitor, using 'presenter view'. What this means is that in front of me I can see the slide the audience sees as well as the next one that's coming. I can also store notes underneath the slide and refer to them if I get stuck and lose my place. Equally, simple cue cards, held in your hand or set out on a table close by will allow you to organize your thoughts and give you some comfort that you're at the right place.

7. **Be Prepared.** I never start a talk even slightly unsure about the time I'm supposed to stop talking. I write the time (and the timing of any breaks) on the agenda, or in the slide notes, so that if someone asks me what time lunch is I have the answer right in front of me, and I'm not trying to answer a question in a fluster. There are several other things to be prepared for. Making sure you've been to the toilet is most important (particularly if, like me, you drink a lot of water when you give talks).

8. **Be Prepared for what you're not prepared for.** Something bad or weird will invariably happen. The laptop will malfunction, there'll be a loud bang in the corridor outside, someone's phone will ring with a ridiculous ringtone. You can't prepare for these eventualities, but you can just remind yourself that they're not going to ruin your day. This leads me on to …

9. **Go with the truth in the room.** OK, that might sound a little weird, so bear with me. The audience holds a universal truth. While everything is working normally, the truth is that they're there for a talk, they're listening to you and so on. But when something goes wrong, the words coming out of your mouth are no longer that truth. If the fire bell goes or a phone goes off and you just try to ignore it and power through, you may think that's the professional response. However, what you've just done is ignored the audience's truth. Making the connection between you and that truth can be magical. So if a phone goes off, just say the word, 'hello'. Or answer their phone. Or just pause and smile. Let the audience know you're connecting with their truth. And perhaps even follow it. Often the most magical moments of truth are the unscripted ones.

10. **Be yourself.** Be confident that what you have to say is interesting, and that the best way to get the message across is as authentically and humanly as possible. Just because you're standing on a stage or at the front of a classroom you don't need to turn into an *X-Factor* star. Put forward the best version of you, not a poor imitation of someone else.

11. Oh, and my bonus tip. If in doubt about what picture to choose for a slide, **choose either cute cats and bunnies**, or a photo that tells the audience something more about you and your relationship with the subject. But cats and bunnies work every time.

Ninja Cheats

▶ For reading lists, remember that 'just enough' is the order of the day, not everything on the list. Don't have time to read this whole section and running out of time? Try reading the 'Mining' section on page 158.

▶ In a massive rush and feeling stressed? Spend ten minutes meditating and clearing your head of the stress before you waste hours rushing around stressed. What you need now is perspective, not panic or procrastination. If you don't know how to meditate, download Headspace or Buddhify onto your phone and take ten minutes letting them help you clear your stress. There's more about meditation on page 140.

▶ Use Rudyard Kipling's famous 'Six Honest Serving Men' to help you with critical thinking and problem-solving: ask what, why, when, how, where and who.

Are you a Study Ninja?

▶ A Study Ninja is Ruthless with information – because there's so much of it, they have to be! They use the 80-20 rule to cut through the unnecessary and find the valuable.

▶ A Study Ninja uses Stealth and Camouflage to protect their Focus, so that they can use their most valuable periods of attention on the hardest tasks without getting interrupted.

▶ A Study Ninja works best when they experience that state of Zen-Like Calm that comes from meditation, clarity and a sense of control over what they're doing.

6. WRITING

WRITING LIKE A TWERP AND WHY THINKING ABOUT SEX HELPS YOU WRITE ESSAYS

'For sale: baby shoes, never worn'

Next time you're agonizing over word limits, it might be wise to remember the famous six-word story above, attributed to Ernest Hemingway, which offers a reminder of the power of words. Chosen wisely, your words have the power to persuade, to invoke strong emotional responses or paint brilliant landscapes. Chosen badly, they infuriate markers and ultimately reduce your grades.

In this chapter we're going to start by looking at what you should know before you start to write and how to plan the perfect essay. Then, for the rest of the chapter, we'll look at the productivity of writing and things you can do to adopt the habits of successful writers (without the 10am whisky drinking, obviously).

FAIL TO PLAN, PLAN TO DICK AROUND ON YOUTUBE.

I have dedicated a whole chapter later in the book to procrastination. That chapter deliberately comes near the end of the book as I want us to have ironed out some of the habits that cause procrastination along the way. But that also means I need to address it as a separate issue here. So before we dive into writing, let's address the planning that should go into an essay, report or assignment. A good dose of Ninja Preparedness here will save you lots of lost hours in the procrastination vortex. One of the scariest things for a writer is the blank page. Staring at a blank page is a terrifying part of every creative process, from writing songs to drawing pictures to writing books. You have nowhere to turn, nothing to cling to and it feels daunting. Facing the blank page with a plan, however, is empowering. So it's important, before you even sit down at your computer or put your hands over the keys of your keyboard, to map out a bit of a process.

PLANNING AN ESSAY THE TWERP WAY

I've always loved being in the flow as a writer, but it's taken me years (and three books) to recognize that writing is a process. I thought I just … wrote stuff. I never really stopped to consider what I was doing. But in recent times as I've reflected on what I do and how I do it, I've realized that I have cobbled together something resembling a process. My process is to write the TWERP way. There are five stages:

THINKING

You'll notice that the first stage doesn't involve any writing at all. This is an important distinction to make. It's especially difficult if you feel up against a deadline to take time out to think about what you should be writing. It feels so urgent that you should 'start'.

The thinking stage is important, and needs to do several things:

1. Bring together the reading or research you've been doing (ideally into one central place – more of which shortly).

2. Start to structure the piece of writing.

3. Generate ideas for the 'scaffolding' (the beginning, middle and end).

4. Generate ideas for some of the key points or even tiny details such as little phrases you might use.

5. Give you the confidence to stare at that blank page.

Only once you've done all of these things are you ready to sit in front of the keyboard. It is my strong suggestion that you use physical pen and paper during the thinking stage. You can use Post-it notes, different colours, mind maps, the backs of envelopes, it doesn't really matter. But separating this out into an activity that you physically can't do at the computer is important. Without that distinction, it can be tempting to begin the writing before you're really ready, and that only leads to getting stuck.

Before you sit down to write, know the story you're trying to tell. Know the beginning, middle and end. Think about the 'struggle' in the middle part of the story – between good and evil, what you think is right and what you think is wrong, darkness and enlightenment.

WRITING

Once you've done some quality thinking, it's time to start writing. Now here's the bit that might freak you out. When you start writing, don't worry about whether it's any good. Seriously. Now let me explain why I say that. Writing sounds like it should be easily the biggest of the five stages. It might be, but in my experience it's usually not at all. Lots of friends and people I've worked with have asked me: 'How long did it take you to write *How to be a Productivity Ninja*?' The short answer is, 'well, I went off the grid for about 3–4 weeks and wrote every day, morning noon and night, until it was done'. So it could be said that I wrote a book in less than a month. But that's misleading for so many reasons. It ignores the two years before that where I was actively thinking about the book and the four or five months after that first draft was done where I was editing, rewriting and polishing. With all three books I've written, I've also engaged focus groups of typical readers to give me their reactions, before doing a final rewrite and polish too. So what most people think of as the writing actually barely even amounts to the first draft.

You'll have plenty of time to edit it later; plenty of time to make those bad words good. You'll also have plenty of time (and a better perspective) to make the thing all hang together. So the worst thing you can do is procrastinate over needing the first draft to be brilliant. Give yourself the permission to write what Natalie Goldberg describes as a 'shitty first draft'. Relieved of that pressure to make it brilliant from the moment you start writing, you can really focus on your ideas and experiment – knowing that you can change it again later – and not crumble under the weight of personal expectations of perfectionism.

EDITING

Editing is different from writing. It requires more of a critical eye. Half of editing is the drudgery of spelling and grammar checking, but the other half of it is about readability. This is a difficult thing to do as you go along, as by its nature it requires you to put yourself in the mind-set of a reader, not a writer. It needs you to read your work as if you're reading it for the first time, and I find personally the only way I can do this is to put some distance between the time I finish writing and the time I start editing. Much like baking a cake or a loaf of bread, the worst time to taste it is the second it leaves the oven: you have to let it sit and let the flavours settle down.

REWRITING

Stephen King has a saying: 'writing is rewriting'. In his book, *On Writing*, he describes how he will write a whole novel, then leave it in a drawer for a couple of weeks before he takes it back out and reads it again as a reader. And then, he says, the work really starts, as he begins editing and rewriting, sculpting the words into something often quite different from what that first draft contained. This is powerful as an approach, because it reinforces that permission to write the 'shitty first draft', safe in the knowledge that you are not yet committing to every word.

I also find that often, to work out what I think about something, it helps to first have something to disagree with. Putting your first ideas down doesn't always mean putting your best ideas down, but it does mean that when you come back to think about them again, you're not starting from a blank page and you're probably starting with something familiar enough that you can shape it to the conclusion you want. This, incidentally, is something I'm passionate about when it comes to productivity too: people are often so paralysed by the idea of finishing before they even start, and the 'something to disagree with' approach is liberating. Essentially, any decision trumps indecision: even if you make the wrong choice, you have something to reverse or undo, which is still easier than having nothing to work with at all.

As I mentioned before, when it comes to writing books, I usually operate a focus group system, where a dozen or so people get to see the first draft (easily the scariest part of the whole process for me) and then they provide feedback. This also leads to lots of rewriting. The more you write and the more you know your audience, the more you develop an instinct for what is going to strike a chord or entertain and what's not. But no matter how good this instinct is, it's frequently still wrong, and it's precisely because you're so entrenched in what you're writing that you can't see the wood from the words. So having someone – anyone! – read your work for the first time will give you a unique perspective. It could be that you swap with someone on your course and you read and critique each other's work, but it could just as easily be your housemate who does Geology or your mum. While there's some benefit in having someone read it who knows the subject matter, what they're really doing here is checking the flow, checking it's readable and honestly describing their experience as a reader.

POLISHING

The final step is polishing. Save references, page numbering, text sizing and formatting until the very last minute. Learn to live with imperfection in the text until then. You may want to compile parts of the bibliography as you go along, but resist the temptation to be distracted by this in the text too much as you work – forget about it looking polished on the screen. That only matters when you press 'print' or 'send' for the final time. The reason for this approach is that when you're writing or editing or rewriting, you really need to have all of your Ninja Focus on the subject matter and the flow of the words, not half an eye picking up rogue extra commas or brackets. Do everything you can to keep the momentum going and resist every task or mouse click that stops the flow of the typing and thinking.

THINGS TO REMEMBER AS YOU WRITE

For the rest of this chapter, I'm going to focus on simple and practical writing tips. We'll start with how to structure your paragraphs, then look at how to make your work 'marker-friendly' and then also look at some writing productivity tips to keep you focussed and balanced along the way. Whether you're writing factual essays or persuasive arguments, there really are some simple rules to the process that will massively improve your ability to write and ensure your words attract more influence and of course, higher marks.

HOW THINKING ABOUT SEX WILL HELP YOUR WRITING

We've already talked about the structure of your work, with a beginning, a middle and an end. So now let's talk about that pesky middle bit, which is usually by far the largest of the three sections. The middle bit is where you're exploring the arguments, presenting the facts, showing the struggle or the journey that you need to complete before you can reach your conclusion. Far from this being one large chunk of words, it's really a collection of paragraphs. And getting a good structure for your paragraphs will help you not just with the planning but with the writing too. To make the perfect paragraph, make it SEX(Y):

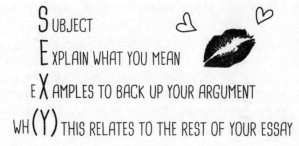

SUBJECT

EXPLAIN WHAT YOU MEAN

e**X**AMPLES TO BACK UP YOUR ARGUMENT

WH**(Y)** THIS RELATES TO THE REST OF YOUR ESSAY

So make each paragraph a little exploration into another idea. Begin each paragraph with the subject matter for that paragraph. Next, explain the idea in more detail and then follow this with examples so that the reader begins to understand the point you're making. Finally, you might finish a paragraph with the 'why', underlining the reason you believe in the idea or have come to the conclusion that you have drawn. So let's say I'm writing a paragraph about Hamlet's indecision in an essay about flawed protagonists in Shakespeare. I might begin with a bold statement like: 'Hamlet's indecisiveness at crucial moments causes his downfall.' Then, I would explain the point I'm making and the consequences indecision had on Hamlet's life. Then, I would provide some examples of particular moments in the story, or even a quote from the text itself, as an example to back up my explanation. And finally, a really great paragraph would link back to why this matters for the rest of the essay, so I might end this paragraph by saying: 'Ultimately, Hamlet's indecisiveness is his fatal flaw, and Fortinbras's focus and determination make him the natural antidote to the "rotten state" of Denmark.' That whole paragraph is really making one distinct point, but then the structure around it adds credibility and evidence for the reader, which makes your arguments easy to understand, believe in – and to give high marks to, of course.

Of course, it's useful to know these rules first so that you can break them, and there will always be exceptions, otherwise your writing would risk becoming formulaic. But writing in this way then makes your job of planning the essay really very easy, because you can plot out the entire essay as one-sentence paragraph openers. You can write out main points you're going to cover in each paragraph, and then this provides the structure for you to build your writing around. Here's an example of how I would structure an essay about how lobbying groups influence government indecision on the issue of climate change – it's simplistic because I'm trying to make it applicable for everyone, but obviously when you write you'll bring your own style and expertise to the table:

> Beginning. My fundamental argument is that lobbying is playing a role in creating chaotic governmental indecision on the issue of climate change and energy security, and that the current political status quo is unable to solve the issue.

1. From the scientific evidence, it is clear that man-made climate change is real.

2. Governments and politicians have an interest in protecting their people and protecting economic interests.

3. Lobbying groups have immense power over politicians.

4. Often there are hidden links between the two groups, such as politicians receiving places on the boards of lobbying groups and oil firms.

5. At the same time, politicians rarely win votes for long-term strategic decision-making and 'short-termism' is prevalent.

6. The short-term profit of the oil and gas industries is favoured above long-term economic stability.

7. It is extremely difficult for the companies to abandon profitable methods, and CEOs risk their jobs when they do so.

8. While it is easy to blame lobbying groups, there needs to be a more joined up solution, which discourages the oil and gas companies from using lobbyists to protect short-term thinking.

9. There is a lack of global leadership and a need for an inspiring figure to bring the parties together with a compelling vision, creating pressure and making lobbying more difficult and less profitable.

10. Leaders such as Bob Geldof (Live Aid), who came from outside the political environment, have been more successful with big campaigns than leaders like Al Gore, who have political 'baggage'.

End. It is clear that lobbying is playing a huge role in creating the chaotic indecision that risks our future sustainability. However, my conclusion is that with a global leadership figurehead who can present a compelling vision for future energy security, the issue might be more easily addressed by politicians and companies because of the public and voter pressure this campaign brought about.

Once I have this structure, each of the sentences (1–10) becomes a paragraph, using the SEX(Y) model. This little bit of planning helps me to then stay focussed on the argument and make sure my points remain on track.

MAKING YOUR MARK ON THE MARKER

Markers have a tough job, but know this provides the key to getting into their good books. Just take a moment to think about how long it takes to critically review your essay. Then think about how many people are also handing in the same essay at the same time. Now think about how many other classes that tutor is teaching. And now you have some idea about the banality of marking that the average teacher or academic is faced with! Achieving top marks happens when you brighten up their day.

One of the best ways to cheer up your tutor is to make your work marker-friendly, so here are ten tips for giving bored and stressed markers what they want:

1. Look pretty for your first impression

Even though the common phrase is 'never judge a book by its cover', markers are already marking your work before they've even read the first words. How your work is set out on the page matters. There are two possibilities here. Firstly, let's assume that your course has issued some kind of style guide, detailing the size of text, the fonts, the spacing and the style you should use. If they have, FOLLOW IT! This is a bugbear of many markers I've spoken to, where students are showing them that they can't follow the simplest instructions. Not a great first impression. Secondly, where there is a little more freedom or vagueness at play (where only a loose style guide exists, say, or none at all), then make sure you use spacing, an easily readable font (Times New Roman is generally considered to be the quickest to read), leave good margins, use regular headings and other such devices to make your work attractive as it sits on the page. First impressions count. Make a good one.

2. Feed them one bite at a time

This is possibly the most important thing to stay aware of as you're writing. A marker is trying to do two things: read your work and then break off from that to think about the marks they're awarding you. By using good spacing, clear paragraphs and good subtitles – depending on what is appropriate for your subject – you allow them to take a breath and do their job, without frustration. Feed them one bite at a time and they won't feel overwhelmed. Splashing the page with a massive blob of text and letting them figure out the structure? You're doomed. Make it easy.

3. Keyword scanning

These next three tips also help to make it easy for your marker. Think about the 'keywords' that a marker might be looking for. If you're working on an essay about research methods into cures for cancer, your marker will likely want to scan down and see if you have included words like *In Vitro*, Oncogenomics or Protodynamic therapy. Luckily, the kinds of words that your marker is scanning for are often words that are easy to spot! Putting these words in the first line of paragraphs (and repeating them in the last line of the paragraph) is a great way to give your marker the confidence to say, 'this person knows this stuff' before they've even digested the first paragraph.

4. Break the flow

The use of bold type, italics, capitals and numbers are all, if used sparingly, great ways to highlight particular words (although you should check to see if your institution has a style guide that prohibits this). Used too much, these things lose their meaning and emphasis and actually have the opposite effect – they make it more difficult to navigate the text and annoy the marker. But slipping one in every page or two should just create that little tiny moment where the reader is forced to break their flow, which when your reader is a marker, allows them an anchor point to come back to while they think about and score your work.

5. Quote

If you're writing about a text, you need to give the message that you're familiar with the original material, so dropping in the occasional quote will add some reassurance. Again, overdoing this technique will be annoying, but a few knowing nods to quotes directly from the text shows that you've done your research and can be trusted in making your arguments.

6. Passion-pandering

Of course, if the person marking your work was also your class teacher or lecturer, you have another secret weapon: pandering to their passion! Think back to the class or review your notes. What was the joke, fact, or the little obsession, where you suddenly felt their passion-level increase? Was there something you could tell they were particularly interested in? Teachers and lecturers are often motivated by wanting to share their passions and ideas with the world, and if you can show that they've made you passionate or interested in what they're saying, that's the best form of job satisfaction they can get. It gives them a warm glow! If you can, establish this by stealth outside of the class, and then you have the basis for an essay that the marker will enjoy reading.

7. Keep it simple

I often find that as I'm writing something I have more thoughts that could easily develop into different directions. Thus, a 1,500 word piece has the potential to career and meander into something closer to 5,000 words. It's not that those other ideas are bad, they're just good for different essays – that you're not writing! So stay Ruthlessly on-topic. Know when you need to rein in your own enthusiasm and keep the narrative structure simple so that you don't risk someone getting lost reading it.

8. Let sub-headings be your guide

One of the most powerful structural weapons you have is the sub-heading. These cunning little mini-titles should act as little signposts through the journey of your narrative. Choose the words carefully because they carry a lot of weight. You can make them occasionally witty and entertaining, but most of all, make sure they carry the reader through the sections, again focussing on the marker's ability to skim-read. Occasionally certain institutions have differing attitudes here about the use of sub-headings – some may encourage them, and others may not permit you to use them at all – but even if you can't use them in the final piece, using sub-headings to aid your own thinking and get clear on the structure of the piece is a great tip (you can always take them out once it's all come together).

9. **Be yourself**

Everyone loves to recognize the human being behind what they're reading. While it's easy to adopt generic styles, adding a little personality to your written work will make it more engaging. To do this, just be yourself. Throw away some of the rules and express what you want to express – and be confident in doing so.

10. **All's well that ends well**

Make sure your first and last paragraphs are well-constructed. The first paragraph should tell the reader clearly what the rest of the essay is going to tell them, while the last paragraph should remind them what you've told them and how you've answered the question. The last paragraph is likely to be the thing that lingers most strongly in the marker's mind as they make their judgement about your mark, so make it clear. If appropriate, make it a rousing and passionate conclusion. Burn fires and light fireworks in their mind.

WRITING PRODUCTIVITY

Writing, particularly if you are engaged in long essays or a thesis, can be a test of mental stamina (and sometimes physical stamina too if you're sitting in one position for too long). It's certainly an attention management challenge. Luckily, we've already made you a Ninja, so here is the Ninja way to handle long writing sessions and still come out on top.

THE TWO-HOUR RULE

When it comes to prolonged periods of writing, I tend to live by the two-hour rule: in any given session of writing, you have at most two hours of proactive attention to 'spend'. Knowing this allows you to quickly realize that spending half that time getting 'warmed up' while you check Facebook messages is a criminal waste. It's not to say that you can't do more than two hours of writing in a day, but I think it's difficult to spend much more than two hours in one sitting, before having at least an hour's break and doing something else to refresh. I wrote a large chunk of this book from a beach hut in Sri Lanka, precisely because I wanted to put in a lot of hours and avoid distractions, but even then, you need to break off from the writing to refresh, otherwise you quickly find that you're spending hours and hours chugging through sub-optimal performance. So give yourself a break, and you'll notice the positive effects.

CLOSE YOUR EYES

Two of the best ways to press the mental reset button and enforce an attention break after a couple of decent hours of writing are naps and meditation. A quick power nap (no more than an hour) will leave you feeling fresh and raring to go again. Meditation is another great way to feel refreshed because it quietens the mind, so you go from thinking about everything in the world, to thinking only of your own breathing in this particular moment.

GET OVER YOURSELF

Napping or meditating in the middle of the day can feel a little naughty. So can eating meals at odd times, or craving a lot of snacks, or skipping your usual exercise routines. It's best to get over the guilt and more importantly, to listen to your own body. Disregard the rules and social conventions. Nap when you want, meditate if you want to, eat at times that suit you – and as long as you're not waking up everyone else in your house, keep whatever routine you choose. Don't feel guilty about any of it, and look after yourself instead.

CONSTRAINTS

Play with constraints. Rather than giving yourself all evening to write, decide that you're going to put in two good hours and then go out. Or go out for the morning and do your writing in the afternoon. This sounds counterintuitive, but it will actually increase your productivity, whereas sitting at the desk all day forcing out that third hour, but getting no rest or Balance in your life is not just inefficient, but it will quickly turn your writing into a joyless chore (and I'm pretty sure if you asked your favourite authors which of their works were produced as a joyless chore, the answer would be 'none'). So play with constraints and mini-deadlines – Balance your day with writing and other things and you'll notice your productivity improving.

POMODOROS AND ATTENTION

You'll remember the Pomodoro Technique, where you work in 25-minute chunks? This is something I use a lot when I'm writing. 25-minute chunks are just enough to get one big section down, or a few key paragraphs. Then you break for five minutes and repeat. Typically I might squeeze five Pomodoros in before I take a longer break, so just slightly more than the two-hour rule.

I'VE STARTED SO I WON'T FINISH

As much as it is useful, the Pomodoro Technique can often be annoying when you're working on something big. The reason is it breaks your flow and forces you to have a five-minute break. 'Ah! How will I know where I was?' is the common fear. It can feel annoying having to get settled back down after your five-minute break and get back into the flow. To make it easier, here's my killer Ninja productivity tip for when you're writing. Never get up to have a break when you've just finished a sentence or section. Get up to go for a break when the cursor is flashing in the middle of a sentence, even in the middle of a word. This will feel really weird at first. But try it and I promise you you'll be amazed at how quickly it gets you back in the zone. Give your mind a place to latch onto as soon as you sit back down, rather than creating the thinking and backtracking that's necessary when you're looking at a completed section and wondering where to go next.

CREATE ACCOUNTABILITY

As we learned earlier in the book, self-control is overrated. We're often happier letting ourselves down than we are letting other people down. Luckily, there are ways you can turn this to your advantage. Create writing partnerships: pairing up with a friend and sitting in a room with your laptops writing is a great way to keep each other focussed, especially to overcome Distant Deadline Deficiency. There are all kinds of writing groups, both in-person and online, where you can sit and write with likeminded people to keep you accountable. You can also ask the people you live with to 'witness' you completing a thousand words, or getting to the end of a piece of work. We hate looking foolish or letting other people down, much more so than we hate letting ourselves down, so create some accountability.

CREATE THE RIGHT ENVIRONMENT

We've talked already in this book about things that help you keep your Ninja Focus. Since writing requires a lot of proactive attention, you need to do everything possible to create the right environment. And allow yourself to indulge your 'inner diva' here to some extent. If you like working on a particular table, or listening to a particular type of music, or like the room to look or feel a certain way, then go for it. Get the environment right – partly because doing so gives you one less excuse to not work!

STAND UP

It's been said that sitting is the new smoking. It's not good for our bodies. Standing desks are now commonplace in many offices, and even available from places like Ikea as the idea of standing at your desk becomes more mainstream. I currently alternate between a standing desk and a sitting one and I find the variety really helps keep me focussed. But more importantly, when I stand up I have much less shoulder tension and back pain, and apparently I'm burning off a lot more calories, too, so that's a bonus!

Scrivener

Scrivener is an alternative to Microsoft Word, Mac's Pages and other word processing apps, and it's what I use when I'm writing. I'm a total fan. It has a few neat features that save a lot of time, particularly if you are writing something that involves a lot of research documents or

chapters. What makes it different? Put simply, it avoids some of the 'fiddlyness' of those other packages. Imagine that instead of writing one document like you do in Word, you have a different document for each chapter, you can create new ones and move them around with ease, and you can save them as one complete piece as well as individually. This allows you to flit from the top to the bottom to the middle of your work easily, and without the continuous scrolling that Word documents necessitate. Underneath all of the chapters I'm writing, I have all my research material so I can refer to it instantly, all of which open as I click them, and then I don't need to close them once I've taken what I need, I just click back to the chapter I'm working on. It's hard to describe or emphasize just how much friction this removes from the writing process, but basically it keeps you firmly in the zone.

It saves your work every ten seconds, without fail. So if ever your computer runs out of juice or crashes, then you know you won't lose any work in the process. I have mine automatically saving my work to Dropbox too, so if I left my computer on a train, or if it was stolen, I'd know my work was safe.

It also has some brilliant settings like the 'distraction free screen' that puts all the settings and other windows you have open in the background and forces you to focus only on what you're writing. And at the end of the process, if your tutor wants the final version in Microsoft Word (or any other file format) it takes a matter of seconds to export the whole thing to a Word document. You can even export your work into e-book format and have it for sale on Amazon within minutes, if you so wish!

Scrivener isn't free – an education licence is £24 at the time of writing – and of course there are many free alternatives, but if you're going to spend so many hours of your life writing essays and compiling research, this probably isn't the place in your life I'd advise scrimping to save £24! Scrivener is available to purchase from www.literatureandlatte.com

EXERCISE: STOP!

OK, stop right there. I want to ask you a question and please be honest with yourself and with me. Did you even for one moment there wonder whether I have been paid by literatureandlatte.com to write such an excellent review of Scrivener and urge you to buy it? Did you?

Why am I asking you this? Because that would mean you're already reading critically like a Study Ninja. And even though I'd be slightly offended that you'd think that of me, I'd be delighted at your critical reading skills at the same time. If that thought didn't remotely cross your mind, you should take notice of this and perhaps revisit the critical reading section in the last chapter.

And just to be completely transparent and answer that question directly, the answer is no: I haven't received any money from the makers of *any* of the apps or products in this whole book. While lots of authors and bloggers do get paid to advertise things, I recommend everything in my books because they're things I use and love.

So hopefully that's all clear, but I'm so glad you asked the question.

PRÉCIS WRITING

Finally, in this chapter, a few (short) words about writing a précis. A précis is a short summary of a longer piece, usually no more than a third of the original passage. Learning to write them is a useful skill to help you understand longer pieces and exercise critical thinking. It's also a useful revision tool. Here are four quick rules to help you write précis quickly and easily:

▶ Read the whole piece first (at least speed-reading, if not feast-reading).

▶ Be clear in your mind what the piece is about, and write the first sentence or two, which should summarize the main point of the piece.

▶ Next, work paragraph by paragraph. If you are writing a précis of your own work, this should be easy, as you're using the first sentence in each paragraph to introduce a new point in each paragraph. So if you've followed this rule, it should be as easy as taking the first sentence of each paragraph and compiling these to make up your précis.

▶ Finally, read your précis from start to finish, making sure that it 'stands up' on its own. You may still need a few little tweaks, edits and polishes.

TWO ADDITIONAL TIPS FOR SUMMARIZING KEY CONCEPTS

Learning to summarize is a valuable transferable skill. Here are two quick tips to get you thinking along the right lines here:

1. Use the 'curious, intelligent six-year-old test'. If you don't know how to explain the concept to an intelligent, curious six-year-old, then you don't understand it. When asked by people who don't like football what the 'offside rule' is, so many people start talking about players being level and two players in front of the goal and various babbly jargon. Using this test, what I say is: 'it's a rule to prevent people just hanging around by the goal, or "goal-hanging", as it's sometimes called.' Get to the nub of *why* this matters.

2. My friend Rosie from the National Union of Students often asks students to summarize an issue in a tweet. Whittling down the

main point(s) to just 140 characters takes discipline – a great example of a constraint being a useful tool.

Ninja Cheats

▶ If you have a big essay to write and you're running out of time, I'd recommend starting with the 'Writing Productivity' section on page 197. This will give you some shortcuts to crack on at maximum speed.

▶ Instead of writing an outline structure of the essay, use the 'SEX(Y)' model by writing the 'subject' sentence for each paragraph. This will give you the structure and then you can fill in the gaps later.

▶ Create accountability – tell someone when your essay will be finished. And then the race is on!

Are you a Study Ninja?

▶ A Study Ninja knows Ruthless Focus is important for writing. This is the time to put other bits of your life on hold (for a few hours or a few days) and rack up the Fun Points to spend when the work is done!

▶ A Study Ninja is Prepared. Tools like Scrivener offer the best possible chance to stay in the zone.

▶ A Study Ninja uses Stealth and Camouflage to protect writing time and avoid interruptions and distractions.

7. MEMORY TECHNIQUES

HOW TO REMEMBER THINGS LIKE A WORLD MEMORY CHAMPION AND WHY THE SPICE GIRLS CAN HELP YOU PASS YOUR EXAMS

When I was kid, I had little need for taxis; my dad made a great chauffeur. Yet from a very young age, even when I couldn't recite my friends' phone numbers, I always knew the number of the Coventry taxi company, Allen's Taxis. Why? Because of their ear-worm of a jingle that played seemingly between every other song on our local radio station. I can still hear it remarkably clearly in my brain now: 'Allen's Taxis, Coventry 5-5-5-5-5-5, Allen's Taxis, Coventry 5-5-5-5-5-5 … You dial we'll driiiiive.' At the moment that you need a taxi number, it's the first thing that pops into your head. Not just a catchy little jingle, but a very powerful money-making machine.

You'll have your own examples from local radio jingles, and of course from TV and the web. A struggling British company called 'Compare the Market' wanted to become the biggest price comparison web-site. So what did they do? They launched an advert with the slogan 'Compare the Meerkat', complete with a strange-looking talking meerkat called Aleksandr, dressed like a History professor and hold-ing court with his own catchphrase: 'Simples!' It sticks in your brain much more, doesn't it?

EXERCISE: MEMORABLE ADS

Close your eyes for a moment and think about the most memorable advertising and marketing you can think of. Think about the most memorable examples you've seen in the last week. And think about the ones like my Allen's Taxis jingle that seem to have been with you since childhood. Just go with whatever springs to mind first. Write a few examples here.

What you chose may say something interesting about your learning style (and it might also tell you how difficult it is to get taxi jingles out of your head, too). You'll remember we talked about learning styles and the 'VAK' acronym back in chapter four. Is what you remembered here most typically visual, aural or kinaesthetic? Did you remember strong visual images like meerkats or logos? Were you more swayed by aural sensations, from little jingles to memorable words, or were you more drawn to ads with more of a story, where you see someone experiencing things, like the one where the dad has a terrible day and everything goes wrong – or perhaps your own experiences of the smells and interactions of tasting promotions (which are both good examples of kinaesthetic memory).

Do the results match your learning style? If it does, this reaffirms that you have a strong preference in the way you learn and remember things, and you'd do well to follow that during this chapter as we talk about memory. And if it didn't? Well, it's actually very common for people to recall examples of all three learning styles. You see, learning styles are just a rough indication of preference, not an indication that your brain is 'closed off' to learning in other ways. And when it comes to memorizing things, we need to use every weapon at our disposal.

So in this chapter we're going to look at simple techniques to make your revision notes come to life and stick in your head. If you're going to remember lots of pointless stuff like talking animals, it may as well be in the pursuit of learning instead of the pursuit of knowing where to get insurance from. We'll look at how the three learning styles affect the memory techniques you should choose, and also why self-testing – not cramming – is the secret to memorizing things ready for exams.

THE NINJA APPROACH TO MEMORY

Much of what we're taught about how to memorize stuff actually ignores quite a lot of scientific evidence. For example, re-reading material, using highlighter pens to identify key information, or rewriting your notes are all things that have been found to have quite a limited impact on your ability to retain information. And conversely, much of what we're not used to or 'never get around to' are exactly the things that make a real difference. So before we look at specific techniques for visual, aural and kinaesthetic learners, this is the seven-step approach to Ninja-level memory:

1. Practise the result, not the practice

In the next chapter we'll talk more about the exam hall, but much of what you're working towards crystallizes in that small number of hours at the end of each term or year. Exams are an artificial environment and one that we should learn to be as comfortable in as possible. Yet in most courses, the opportunities available to replicate exam conditions and practise the bit that gets you the results are limited. You're encouraged to practise everything else: revision is set up around practising note-taking, practising being at home studying in relaxed conditions, practising reading … all of which don't happen in an exam hall. And you'll write for an hour here or there, but never timing yourself under the conditions of the exam, which is three hours long.

Here are a couple of huge secrets of academia, too: there are only so many questions you can ask about certain topics. There are only a small number of ways to test the same knowledge. And guess what? The people who write the tests are humans too, and just as lazy as you or me. So if you thought that past papers were yesterday's news, think again. They hold the key to your success. The more past papers you sit down and take, in controlled exam-like conditions, the more you'll practise the skill of sitting in an exam room and operating under exam-like conditions. Choosing the questions to tackle, monitoring and prioritizing your time, and working in a concentrated and uninterrupted way are all things that need practice, yet to do this only when your teacher stages a mock exam is crazy. Choosing to spend time doing the things that are proven to be less successful (reading, rewriting notes, highlighting sections of text) instead of doing more exam practice is beyond crazy.

2. Self-testing and getting over yourself

Self-testing is one of the most under-rated habits that a student of anything can pay more attention to. Robert Bjork and Nate Kornell's 2007 paper

for the Psychonomic Bulletin and Review looked at the study habits of college students in the USA, and found that students doing sim-ple tests on themselves regularly rather than just reading the mater-ial were more successful, yet only about two-thirds of students quiz themselves at all, and most only when faced with an upcoming exam, rather than as a regular habit. A 2012 paper by Marissa Hartwig and John Dunlosky for the same journal asked students in the middle of their courses about their study habits and their current grade aver-ages, and found that – surprise, surprise – there was a direct correla-tion between the students who regularly quizzed themselves and the ones with the higher grade averages.

This experience is something we see in many other areas of life, too. We can get lost in the fear of failure, which makes it difficult for us to face the prospect of a test (even one where the only per-son who will see the result is ourselves!). So it's more comfortable to sit and read the same information over and over again than to ask ourselves the question: 'OK, what do I know so far?' For the same reason, software developers talk about releasing the 'minimum via-ble product', rather than waiting for something to be perfect. Why? It's not because they like releasing software with bugs in it that will inevitably annoy or disappoint people. It's because they know that only by having that feedback about what's missing can they work towards the mythical holy grail of perfection. And focussing on what they have got rather than on all the reasons it's not 'ready' empowers them to release something into the world now. The same is true for your learning. Don't worry about what you don't know yet, but work out how far you've come. Test yourself. Create situations where you need to explain it to your friends or family. Make a PowerPoint or flashcard presentation that you perform in front of the mirror. Pretend you're an expert already.

And when there are things that you don't know the answer to? That is where to focus your future study. This is known as 'self-correction', and it's one of the most powerful tools you have to help you learn. The more you can create opportunities to test and apply your knowledge, the more you create the opportunities to self-correct. The results of the tests don't matter, but the act of testing what you know will help your brain piece together what you do know and identify where the work is needed. (And you'll be surprised if you do this regularly just how much of it begins to stick.)

3. **Clear your brain**

There's a reason we started this book with making sure you're organized. Memory and learning requires Ninja Focus. Sitting down to study with a hundred other things on your mind (whether they be relationship troubles, a nagging family member, or a decision you need to make) will make it difficult to produce periods of deep concentration. So before you sit down to learn, you need to clear that gunk out of your brain. It may only take a few seconds, but practise some Ninja Mindfulness. You could use it as a chance to run through those questions we talked about, such as 'How am I feeling?', and to identify what's going on in your life emotionally, outside of your studies. And then, turning to your studies, think about the DUST of procrastination: identifying what's Difficult, Undefined, Scary or Tedious in what you're about to sit down to do. We lose so many needless hours to worry, poor attention and mindlessly staring at words on a page, yet a few choice minutes or even seconds at the beginning of a session can give you the clarity to use your attention more wisely.

4. Train your brain

Your brain is a muscle. It can be developed, exercised and improved. We often tend to think of our brains as a kind of static receptacle, a bit like a computer hard drive that we're adding knowledge or information to (until presumably one day it's full!), but our brains are more dynamic than this. The flexibility of our brains and the way they learn new things is called 'neuroplasticity', and its effects and the science behind neuroplasticity makes compelling reading. But long story short: we can make different connections in the brain and effectively 're-wire' the way we think.

A famous study of neuroplasticity conducted MRI scans of the brains of London taxi drivers to look at the hippocampus, an area of the brain that deals with memory and navigation. London cabbies need to learn 'The Knowledge', which basically means knowing every London street off by heart; a process that usually takes around two years to complete. The study found that over the course of learning 'The Knowledge', the drivers' hippocampi became generally larger than similar-aged healthy males. So as the brain makes more connections, it gets stronger and even changes shape! If you wanted to be physically stronger you'd join a gym, and when it comes to the brain, there are a number of great ways to train, re-train and get stronger.

If you want to have more proactive attention and concentrate for longer, you can practise meditation; if you want to improve your self-control for studying, then meditation or the development of other habits (like a short morning exercise) will help you grow your self-control muscle; at my company, Think Productive, we've used the teaching of improvised comedy to improve creativity and on-the-fly decision-making among our staff; and if you want to improve memory, problem-solving and information-processing, you can play games like Sudoku, practise memory techniques and quizzes or just let your mind wander towards making new connections by watching creative TED talks online, or going for a long walk. There are also a number of dedicated apps developed by neuroscientists that you can use to improve your performance.

Lumosity

Lumosity is a fantastic brain training app, which you can play for free on their website (www. lumosity.com) as well as via your smartphone or tablet. You can access enough for free to get a good idea for some of the types of games and mental 'workouts' that you can do to help. And  for just a few pounds a month, you can get fuller access, play more games and practise harder. The whole app is designed to act like a mental personal trainer, so the more you play, the harder the games get. Often as you play, you experience getting into a groove where it feels easy, followed by moments of 'brain freeze' where you're totally confused if you think about things too hard. If your idea of working out is playing fun and strangely addictive little games, then this is for you!

5. **Train your body**

Regular exercise improves mental performance. One of the reasons for this is because exercising releases a protein in the brain called 'brain-derived neurotrophic factor' (BDNF for short) which is known to promote healthy nerve cells in the brain. Studies into BDNF have found clear links between high levels of BDNF and improved memory and recall. Fifteen to twenty minutes is all you need to make a difference: a quick run or cycle, lifting a few weights or an aerobic workout in front of a DVD. As well as improving memory and recall, a study in the British Journal of Sports Medicine also found remarkable changes in heat maps of the brain, showing a huge jump in the level of brain activity after even such a small period of physical warm up.

A Study Ninja doesn't need hours and hours down the gym or to be running marathons (both of which I can vouch for as extremely pleasurable activities, but ones that can be difficult to fit sustainably into a busy routine). It will almost feel like cheating, but doing what can seem like no more than a quick burst is all you need.

6. **Little and often**

The same short burst principle should be your approach to sitting down to study. We talked earlier about the effect of primacy and recency, where the brain finds it easier to remember the first and last bits of information more easily than the bits in the middle. And we also talked about the Pomodoro Technique, which works by instilling the habit of breaking after 25 minutes (rather than waiting until our brain naturally breaks its attention span, typically at around 40–45 minutes). It can be tempting to make a virtue of sitting down for hours at a time, but realistically, all you are doing is operating on diminishing returns – when even a short break is enough to get you back to peak performance. So if you want to design the perfect afternoon of study, think 'little and often'.

The same 'little and often' rule should apply to how you design a term or a year, giving your brain ample opportunities to process new information (which your brain often does while you sleep). Study after study has shown that learning is best conducted in short bursts over longer periods of time.

7. **Avoid cramming**

Cramming, the art of leaving it all to the last minute and then stuffing your brain full of information at just the right time, is not completely without merit. It can be useful in the final days before exams, but will be much more effective if what you're doing by that stage is looking for a final bout of immersion in the subject, rather than trying to give yourself a crash course because you slacked off earlier in the year.

The worst form of cramming is cramming the night before an exam. Any benefits from cramming are quickly outweighed by the negative impact that sleep deprivation will have on your judgement and mental performance during the exam.

PRACTISE, PRACTISE, PRACTISE

All seven of these approaches require practise to develop them as habits. But like the development of any habit, the more you do it the easier it becomes. So making these things as natural as possible and part of your day-to-day life is key. It's easy to turn on the style a week or two before exams come. And of course it's easier to perform when you know the pressure is on than it is in those heady days of Distant Deadline Deficiency, but the more you get into habitual routines, the less willpower it requires to keep good habits alive.

VISUAL MEMORY TECHNIQUES

THE JOURNEY METHOD

This is the ultimate in visual memory tech-niques. It takes a fair amount of practice, but the rewards are huge. In fact, various versions of this technique are what's used by all the world memory champions to achieve phenomenal results, such as being shown an entire deck of cards, card by card, and then being able to recall each card in order – and if these techniques can be used to memorize entire decks of cards (the most boring data there is!) then they can easily be used to remember the dates of wars or the elements of the periodic table.

The journey method works by acknowledging that our brains only have a limited capacity for remembering standardized and unre-markable information, particularly in specific orders. So how do you improve memory and recall of the information? You make the visual images stronger in your mind, and structure them by tying them to particular points on a journey.

Before you can start to create 'journeys' of useful information, you need to get a clear vision in your mind about a journey you know well. A good example of this might be the walk from your house to your school or university campus, or it could be the car journey from home to work or a walk from your bed to the kitchen in your house.

It can be any journey where you can pinpoint the sequential points along it. So here's a twelve-point journey from my house to my office, which I regularly do on my motorbike.

1. The doorstep

2. The bus stop outside my house

3. The bingo hall at the bottom of my road

4. The traffic lights next to the pub and antique shop

5. The corner where my road meets the sea

6. Brighton SeaLife Centre

7. Brighton Pier

8. The Grand Hotel

9. The Park

10. The traffic lights where I turn right

11. The parking space where I park my bike

12. The front door of my office

Now, I have to place the things I want to remember along the route of this journey. So for example, if I had to remember the popular twelve days of Christmas, I would imagine each of the twelve things from the song, associated with strong visual images at each point of the journey. Here's what I imagined for each stage:

1. **A partridge in a pear tree.** The comedy character Alan Partridge, sitting on my doorstep, eating a pear.

2. **Two turtle doves.** Two teenage mutant ninja turtles standing at the bus stop.

3.   **Three French hens.** A large hen, holding a baguette with a string of onions around her neck, standing outside the bingo hall.

4.   **Four calling birds.** A tiny taxidermy bird on a massive 1980s mobile phone, for sale in the window of the antique shop.

5.   **Five gold rings.** Mo Farah, the Olympic gold medallist, holding up five gold medals on the corner next to the sea.

6.   **Six geese a-laying.** A shabbily dressed man with a cardboard sign saying 'geese a job', waiting for the SeaLife Centre to open.

7.   **Seven swans a-swimming.** A man wearing a Swansea City Football shirt, a snorkel, a pair of swimming goggles and some flippers, about to jump off Brighton Pier for a swim.

8.   **Eight maids a-milking.** One of the stars of *Made in Chelsea*, drinking milk while sat in the suitably glamorous location of the bar of the Grand Hotel.

9.   **Nine ladies dancing.** The Spice Girls, dancing one of their routines in the middle of the park.

10. **Ten Lords a-leaping.** Lord Sugar, the star of the BBC show *The Apprentice* (who is known, among many other things, for being quite short in height), jumping up so that he can be seen above the railings next to the traffic lights.

11. **Eleven pipers piping.** The former Warwickshire cricket player, Keith Piper (who was once banned from playing for testing positive for cannabis), sat in my parking space, smoking a pipe and preventing me from parking.

12. **Twelve drummers drumming.** The drummer from my favourite band, Hiatus Kaiyote, fiercely practising a drum solo on a drum kit on the steps of my office.

Each of the images are designed to be remarkable, so the funniest, rudest or just plain strangest images are what work well – if I just imagined five gold rings, or two turtle doves, I'd be much less likely to commit the images to memory because they're more normal things. Another useful tip here is to imagine people or characters, because unlike static objects, people can move and interact with the places on your journey.

RE-USING THE JOURNEYS

Obviously, associated with each point on that journey is a very memorable image. This is what helps you to remember the information visually. But that also creates a small problem: now that I'm imagining the Spice Girls dancing in the middle of the park, it's harder to think of the park as a blank canvas again, ready to remember the next thing. Different experts will tell you different things here: Dominic O'Brien, a world memory champion, has talked about the idea of each journey being like a rewritable DVD. So you can store one or perhaps two sets of information on each journey, but then to remember more sequences, you need to 'wipe the disc' and stop associating that journey with those particular images. So this means you need to have multiple journeys that you can use. This approach is often called the 'memory palace' approach, with the idea that you can imagine lots of different palaces, each with differently styled rooms, although personally I find that real places and real journeys feel easier for me to remember.

EXERCISE: CREATING YOUR JOURNEY

1. First, let's find some information that you really want to remember. How many items are there in your list to remember?

2. Now, imagine a regular journey, and break it down into as many steps as there are pieces of information to remember.

3. Take the first item from your list and turn something from the words or phrase into a character, person, animal or strange image. Imagine the character interacting with the first place on your journey.

4. Do this for each of the next steps of the journey.

5. Now, self-test. Follow the journey and notice which images don't stand out so much. Consider changing the image, or spend a few seconds creating more interaction between the place on the journey and the character who is there. Creating a movement or action can help.

6. Go through and rehearse the journey again – and you're done! Go through this journey again in a day or so and see what sticks.

You can actually use the character and 'remarkable image' technique here, without journeys, to remember all kinds of little things, from passwords to PINs. I use it particularly to remember names, which I'm generally really terrible at. Say for example I'm working with a new group of ten people, I will ask each person their name and as I'm talking to them, try to assign an odd little image to them. So if someone is Catherine I will imagine a cat sitting on her head. For a Derek, I might imagine Ricky Gervais's character of Derek giving them a piggyback, or if someone is Neal I might imagine them kneeling down, or if someone is Shiva I might imagine them dressed up as the cartoon character She-ra, making a 'v' sign with their fingers. Anything that can quickly create a remarkable and strong image in your mind is great.

For numbers, dedicate a picture to each number. One could be a magic wand, two a swan, three a pitchfork, four a sailing boat, five the hook of Captain Hook's hand, six a tennis racquet, seven a cliff edge, eight a snowman, nine a balloon on a string and zero a football. For remembering multiple digits, you can create little stories from these pictures, so the number '8714' would be a snowman, standing on the cliff edge, until he's poked with a magic wand and falls onto a sailing boat. This is a great way to instantly remember dates, PIN numbers and sequences of events.

In fact, for any difficult word, citation or fact that you need to remember, just play around in your mind creating the oddest, weirdest pictures you can possibly imagine. The more you do this, the quicker it gets, and it can make learning dull sequences of facts or information strangely enjoyable.

SMALLER, SMALLER, SMALLER

Particularly if you're a visual learner, a great technique is to look to compress the information into smaller and smaller spaces. This isn't about how small you write it, but the way you compress and summarize whole concepts into acronyms, pictures, diagrams and charts. Think particularly about how you lay it out on the page – as a visual learner, words, pictures and shapes will stick in the memory. When you get into exams or situations where you need to recall the information, you should be able to see the words or pictures connected to each other on the page. For this reason, mind maps are particularly effective for compressing and summarizing information.

DRAW PICTURES

Challenge yourself to turn all of your notes into pictures. It doesn't matter if you can't draw at all – stick men and scribbly pictures of cats and houses will do! – but the idea is to get rid of words and say as much in pictures as possible. Of course, it's possible to cheat here if there are odd words that you really can't think of any pictures to represent them (or things that you know you can't draw!) but setting yourself the challenge will help the visual part of your brain to absorb the information.

GO WITH THE FLOW CHARTS

For anything that involves sequences, use flow charts to map it out from start to finish. Again, it helps visually if you can see a journey on paper, and particularly if you can see interactions between different points of the flow chart (so a flow chart mapping the Second World War might have Hitler or Churchill stepping from one incident to the next, so that you visualize their involvement and influence in the various events.

WATCH TV

Depending on your course, you may find good documentaries, study DVDs and online material that you can sit back and enjoy. But before you put your feet up and crack open a beer, make sure you are genuinely learning, and keeping the balance right between passively watching things and more actively playing with, manipulating and absorbing information. Watching an hour online at the end of a long day of study can be a great way to cement learning as well as providing yourself with some all-important variety.

FLASH CARDS

Flash cards can mean physical cards as well as online note-taking equivalents. Another option here is to use PowerPoint to make simple flashcards. The 'Slide Sorter' view in PowerPoint (Keynote calls this 'Light Table' view) is a great way to order things, move things around and spot patterns between different pictures, diagrams and words. My company, Think Productive, gives talks and presentations at some of the biggest companies and organizations around the world. One of our rules of thumb for making a great presentation is to use no more than about ten words on any PowerPoint slide. This is in stark contrast to how most people use PowerPoint, hiding behind the slides and revealing six or seven bullet points with each slide. But slides full of pictures, or just a single word, or a neat combination of a picture and just a few words are much more memorable. So this little rule of thumb means you can genuinely flash them in front of your face rather than ending up with flashcards that are just smaller cardboard versions of your notebook pages.

CHANGE THE VIEW

Finally as a visual learner, think about your view. I mentioned earlier that it can really help your visual memory to sit in different parts of the classroom for different classes. Your brain will remember slightly more by thinking; 'Oh, that was the lesson when I sat right at the front!' The same is true when you're memorizing things: 'Oh, that was the topic I memorized while sat at the top of the hill!' Or in the loft. Or in the corner of your bedroom. Or in the coffee shop down the road. Again, variety of view keeps your mind fresh and gives you (literally) another angle to hook your learning on. We are creatures of habit, so if we use the same place regularly (our desk at home, a room of hot-desks, the library study areas) we tend to look for similar spots or even the exact same spot time and again, so break this predictability and give your brain more to work with.

Those are a few techniques that are particularly useful for visual learners, but remember, everyone is capable of learning with every learning style, and no-one is a hundred per cent made up of one learning style either. So even if you don't class yourself as a visual learner, try some of those techniques and see what works for you.

AURAL MEMORY TECHNIQUES

Now, let's move on to some of the aural learning techniques, again starting with the most powerful and universal: mnemonics.

MNEMONICS

Let me tell you my very easy method just sums up nine planets. I just did.

My – Mercury

Very – Venus

Easy – Earth

Method – Mars

Just – Jupiter

Sums – Saturn

Up – Uranus

Nine – Neptune

Planets – Pluto

This is an example of a mnemonic, which in this case shows the order of the planets in terms of their distance from the sun (and as long as you ignore the fact that Pluto is a bit contentious these days). In the same way that the journey method and many of the visual learning techniques we've just talked about work by focussing on remembering something other than what you're actually trying to memorize, this works with the aural part of the brain. Remembering short sayings or phrases helps to link the words and help you fill the gaps. Another very common example is 'every good boy deserves football', which musicians are taught to remember the lines on the treble clef.

Creating mnemonics is something that gets easier with practice, but can be a fun way to memorize important data.

EXERCISE: MNEMONICS

1. Pick some information you'd like to memorize (if you don't have anything to hand, you can use the letters 'C.B.B.M.T.C.W.H.W.').

2. Start to notice any patterns in the starting letters, or in the information.

3. Build your phrase around the most unusual patterns of letters, or around more limited letters like 'z' or 'x' (try to resist the temptation to resort to xylophones or zoos, which are easy ways to use those letters, but if you have lots of different mnemonics, it's helpful for them not to be too similar to each other).

4. Use adverbs if you can't think of a verb or noun (words like 'very', 'great', 'small') as a great way to burn up annoying consonants.

5. Once you've pieced together the letters and made a phrase, tell it as a story in your mind (and if you're sat somewhere private, read it aloud, so that your brain can actually hear the vibrations of the sound, too).

The example I gave you was 'C.B.B.M.T.C.W.H.W.', which is because I wanted to remember the order of the last nine British Prime Ministers. I wanted to make sure I could differentiate between Blair and Brown, so I used Blair's name in what I came up with, along with Cameron's:

'CAMERON BOUGHT BLAIR MY TINY CAT WHICH HE WANTED'

So that's how I now remember the order: Cameron, Brown, Blair, Major, Thatcher, Callaghan, Wilson, Heath, Wilson. Since Cameron once described himself as the 'heir to Blair', I like the image of Cameron trying to suck up to Tony Blair, especially with such a ridiculous gift as a tiny cat!

SINGING NOTES

Turn your notes into music. Take the information you want to learn, and think about the catchiest songs you know (these could be songs that you love, or equally could be annoying ear-worm pop songs that you despise. Who knows, if you choose some of the latter and then they help power you to Study Ninja status, maybe you'll even grow to love those songs in the end! For substantial chunks of information, you might want to choose a song with memorable verses as well as a catchy chorus, but equally there are enough songs in the world that you could just focus on catchy choruses. If you're struggling to know what to use, the Beatles were the original masters of the catchy tune, and songs like 'Can't get you out of my head' by Kylie Minogue are not only catchy, but they issue the brain with a subliminal plea (!).

My British Prime Ministers list goes quite well to Carly Rae Jepsen's annoying song 'Call me maybe'. I guess if the music industry will insist on making songs as banal but insanely catchy as that one, at least we can use such evil for good. So our new version goes like this:

> Hey, Cameron Brown Blair,
> And Major Thatcher
> Call-a-ghan Wilson,
> Heath and Wilson.

DON'T READ, TALK

You'll remember that we talked earlier about sub-vocalization during reading – the process by which we hear our own voice inside our head as we read things out. For speed-reading, one of the critical skills is to learn to read without hearing that voice in your head, but this also means that if you're an aural learner, you'll need to read more *slowly* – to feast-read – to give yourself the indulgence of that voice inside your head.

If possible, go one stage further than this, by actually reading aloud. Obviously, don't do this on the bus or in the quiet of the library or you'll risk annoying everyone, but in the comfort of your own home, you'll find that you improve retention and recall of information by hearing those words. The rhythm, pitch, pace and pauses of the information will all help.

RECORD AND LISTEN

Even better than simply reading aloud is to record things and play them back. Everyone can do this on their smartphone, and if you start to find that you're building up quite a large store of information, why not use an old MP3 player (or buy a cheap one for a few pounds online) and fill it with the sound of your own voice reading back useful information for you to memorize. And when you get sick of your own voice, you might also find audiobooks that may help, or you could throw the text onto your Kindle and let the narration feature do the rest. The beauty of this technique is that it makes it easier for you to revise from anywhere: you can take your notes with you to the gym, walking down the street, or even take them to bed with you.

CLOSE YOUR EYES

Repeating facts with your eyes closed is another great technique. By 'shutting down' your most dominant sense, you heighten your sense of sound, which allows you to play to your strengths as an aural learner.

GROUP DISCUSSIONS

Finally, don't underestimate the learning potential of group discussions or book clubs. Hearing other people explaining facts or viewpoints and participating in such discussions brings what you're learning to life and offers opportunities to take your learning off the page – vital for aural learners.

One thing to bear in mind is that group discussions, while helping you identify what you do know, may also throw up gaps in your knowledge. When this happens, be sure to use questions to tease the answers out of other people. Never sit there worrying that everyone knows loads more than you. And

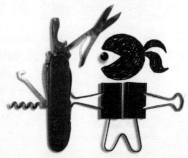

when you're done, make sure you go back through your notes and fill in the gaps. Remember, self-testing is an absolutely critical component of successful learning.

KINAESTHETIC MEMORY TECHNIQUES

Statistically, kinaesthetic learners make up a much smaller population of learners in general than either visual or aural learners, so if you are a kinaesthetic learner, chances are you've also adapted to lots of visual and aural learning techniques, because school classrooms tend to work towards the majority view. What that means is that you're probably already more successful operating outside of your learning preference than others. It also means that you have some secret weapons at your disposal that might propel you to the next level!

We've already talked about group discussions and book clubs. These are vital for kinaesthetic learners, because they create real-life experiences from the information. Flashcards, too, because making things, holding them and moving them around can be fantastic tools as well. And for the same reason, some of the aural techniques such as recording yourself reading out loud or singing facts as lyrics for songs offer opportunities for *experiences*. A kinaesthetic learner has their senses awakened when they can touch and experience things rather than just seeing dull pages of facts, so let's talk about a few other techniques that are particularly useful for developing kinaesthetic memories:

BODY PEGS

This is essentially the journey method but for kinaesthetic learners. Instead of imagining the images of journeys in your mind, you bring the experience to the body. To start with, you need to learn the order of twenty points of the body (much like we did when we identified the stages of the journey). There are various models online for doing this, but this one is perhaps the clearest because numbers 1–9 go across the body and then 10–20 go down the body, as follows:

1 – Fingers of right hand

2 – Palm of right hand

3 – Right elbow

4 – Right shoulder

5 – Top of head

6 – Left shoulder

7 – Left elbow

8 – Palm of left hand

9 – Fingers of left hand

10 – Eyes

11 – Nose

12 – Mouth

13 – Ears

14 – Chest

15 – Tummy

16 – Bum

17 – Right knee

18 – Left knee

19 – Right foot

20 – Left foot

Then, once you remember the twenty 'pegs', your job is to create memories that relate to the things you want to remember, in much the same way as we did with the journey method. The difference this time is that if you want to remember things kinaesthetically, you need your body to interact with the memory prompt as much as possible. So for example, if I was trying to remember 'A partridge in a pear tree', I might start my sticking my right hand fingers into Alan Partridge's mouth and feeling him chew on them as he tries to talk in his funny voice, or imagine holding and biting into a pear with my right hand. Or if I was trying to remember 'Cameron' from my list of British Prime Ministers, I might imagine holding a camera – or simply punching David Cameron in the face. The key here is to interact with each of the objects you choose using senses, emotions and lively experiences.

Again, once you have been through and established all twenty items (or finished your list if it's less than twenty) you should go through it in your mind and self-test. What images aren't sticking? Do you need to change those, or think about them in a slightly different way? And once that's done, give it a day or so and then revisit it to see if it's stuck in your brain.

FUN WITH POST-IT NOTES

Post-it notes offer a useful way for the kinaesthetic learner to experience information in different spaces. The classic stereotype is the student who puts notes up around the house or on the back of the door so they see it before they leave. However, the aim here isn't to discover information by chance or have it sink in by osmosis. It's important to be intentional with how you use Post-its. Here are a few ideas:

▶ Make a set of Post-its on a particular theme and spend time actively running over the information as you stick them up.

▶ Spend time just walking around the room, revising and memorizing what's on them (don't just pin them to the wall and hope for the best).

▶ Group topics together by using different coloured Post-its, or by grouping them in sections on walls.

▶ Combine using Post-it notes with the journey method (so drawing pictures and creating journey points within your own house).

You can then start rehearsing the journey without even needing to walk around the room, but knowing that any time spent in any of those rooms will help cement the learning. Be careful when doing this not to have so many journeys on the go at any one time that you get confused or mix them up.

MAKING IT REAL

Anything you can do to bring learning to life is well worth the time spent. For example, if you are studying the Second World War, consider taking a flight to an important site for a weekend or visit war museums and monuments. If you are studying chemistry, try to recreate experiments (observing all the necessary safety procedures, of course!) and if you can get course mates involved, create roleplays, opportunities for presentations and anything else that brings the facts and dry details to life.

TAKE A LOT OF BREAKS

Finally, as a kinaesthetic learner, it's important to take a lot of regular breaks. The golden Ninja memory rule of 'little and often' is even more important for you, since much of what happens when you're sat at a desk is steeped in learning styles which are not your biggest strength. So make even more of an effort to take regular breaks and keep your body moving, and you'll keep your motivation levels up.

MAKING IT ALL EASIER

In the final part of this chapter, we're going to look at a few quick tips that make all of the above much easier. These are the random little brain hacks that will propel you to memory super-stardom.

CHUNKING

Memorizing information in chunks. For numbers, break them down and look for patterns. For dates or lists, find any groupings that mean you can concentrate on smaller areas of the topic. The more you can break it down, the easier it becomes.

CHEWING GUM BEATS COFFEE

Weirdly, chewing gum releases chemicals in the brain that researchers call 'mastication-induced arousal' (stop laughing, this is serious). Basically, chewing gum is a physical activity for which the brain has prepared physical responses. So because the body is expecting to digest food, it creates an aroused response which produces more alertness for approximately twenty minutes. So five minutes before you're about to embark on your most difficult work, start chewing.

It will actually make you more alert than caffeine will, so it's better than having another coffee or Red Bull!

DON'T CRAM, SLEEP

At the start of this chapter, we looked at seven important rules for Ninja Memory, one of which is 'little and often' and the final one of which was 'don't cram'. There is of course always a place for working hard and focussing on a lot of information in the run-up to a test, but sleep plays an important part in developing memory (quite apart from the fact that sleep aids mental alertness during the test itself, of course).

A study at Harvard gave different groups of students some images to memorize. One of the groups was tested on their memorization after twenty minutes, the other after twelve hours and the last after twenty-four hours. While you might assume that those who had seen the images only twenty minutes earlier would do the best when they were tested, actually they did the worst. And those ones that did the best were those who had had the whole twenty-four hours, because they had the chance to let the images 'sink in'.

Why? Because your ability to retain information works in three different ways: acquisition, consolidation and recall. While the first and last of these occur while you're awake, you need sleep to aid consolidation. As you sleep, you brain is processing information that you couldn't have processed during the day, and rehearsing and regurgitating things that you've been learning (this is why you might sometimes have weird dreams that seem to throw up little details from what you've been doing that day, or why if you've been working hard all day, your dreams seem to be about work somewhere along the line).

So if you're in a position where you really, really need to cram, you have little choice but to cram. But cram until 24 hours before, and then make sure you have either a normal amount of sleep or even a slightly longer one on the night before the test. Far better doing those final couple of hours in the morning after a good night's sleep than staying up later and jeopardising your brain's ability to consolidate your learning.

NINJA PREPAREDNESS: THE RULE OF THREE

I hope the message coming through loud and clear here is that 'little and often' beats cramming, and that self-testing and memorizing over a longer period of time isn't just a 'nice to have', but actually scientifically more effective than allowing the Lazy, Scatterbrained you to leave it all until the last minute. Even without the science, we probably know that this is a better approach. Deep down, we certainly also know that the 'little and often' approach allows for less stress and more smugness. So why do we ignore what's good for us and leave ourselves in the position where we need to cram anyway?

I think part of the problem is Distant Deadline Deficiency. You see, we all have some control over our time and what we choose to do in the quieter weeks of term (or, I should say, the weeks filled with fewer obligations!). So our Lazy, Scatterbrained version of ourselves can win out because the Clever, Motivated version of ourselves doesn't have a particularly good reason for us to employ the 'little and often' approach.

'There's no *deadline*,' says the Lazy, Scatterbrained you, 'so what's the rush?'

But here's one way to flip that psychology around. While we don't always acknowledge it, there's a direct correlation between the hours we're supposed to spend in classes and the hours we're supposed to spend self-studying, and we know that cramming is really just the shifting of a huge proportion of those hours from being spread evenly and nicely throughout the term to being done in concentration as the deadlines approach. So what we need is a thousand mini-deadlines along the way, working alongside our Daily Ritual or Weekly Checklist habits from chapter two.

So here's a way to proactively plan the 'little and often' approach, and override the laziness to wait until the big deadlines: use the power of three. For every hour you spend in class, you should think of that as one of three hours you need to spend on that material. That means, for every hour in class, you have two hours more to complete. Now, you have a new mini-deadline at the end of every class session. Within a day or within a week, plan to spend two additional hours with that topic.

In a school or college, that means you could do an hour of reading before the class and an hour of note-taking and memorizing afterwards. Or you could choose to do both of your hours after the class if there's not too much reading to do beforehand.

In a university degree, where a seminar might follow a lecture, treat the lecture and seminar as two distinct sessions, so you have two more hours to make the lecture up to three (usually an hour's reading before the lecture followed by note-taking and self-testing afterwards) and then the same for the seminar (perhaps an hour reading and preparing for the seminar and another hour writing up notes, memorizing and self-testing once the seminar is done). There might be the odd economy of scale in there, an hour or so that you can skip, but as a general rule of thumb, practise the power of three.

Ask yourself at the beginning of every day or every week: 'How am I going to take each of these hours in class and convert them from one to three?' Use the power of three to give yourself a constant kick up the backside.

Ninja Cheats

▶ If you're short on time before the exam, remember that your memory is limited. Adopt a 'cut your losses' policy – don't try to cram the entire course in a couple of evenings, but rather focus on your strengths and build up good sections of knowledge that you expect may feature in the exam. Panicking now won't improve your memory, so see the situation realistically.

▶ Don't cram the night before. Focus instead on arriving at the exam having slept properly. This will get you a better performance.

▶ On the morning of the exam, eat breakfast for fuel … and then cram as much as you can!

Are you a Study Ninja?

▶ A Study Ninja manages their emotions and tries to remain in a state of Zen-like Calm as much as possible, knowing that this calmness will lead to better memory and better performance.

▶ A Study Ninja is Weapon-savvy and uses the memory techniques that best suit their style, whether it's singing annoying songs or developing warped and weird visual journeys – or something even stranger!

▶ A Study Ninja uses Stealth and Camouflage to increase concentration and keep their attention on the right things.

8. EXAMS

HOW TO SURVIVE THEM AND WHY YOU SHOULD IGNORE THE LIZARD THAT WANTS YOU TO FAIL

Exams, tests, assessments. Whatever it is you're learning there will probably be a time that you're obliged to have someone watch you sit in a room and demonstrate what you've learned, either to be judged immediately, or sent away for judgement. Sitting exams is something that's difficult to avoid and it's an odd and artificial situation. You can certainly practise answering past papers in controlled environments, but like a footballer in a penalty shoot-out, it's just psychologically different when you go from practice mode to the real thing. So in this chapter, we'll focus on the psychology of exams, the practical preparation you need to do for them, and how to survive exam periods without all the stress (or at least without most of it).

THE LIZARD INSIDE YOUR HEAD

Of course, what makes a real exam different from a practice paper is that suddenly there's something important riding on the result, beyond simply your own testing of your learning. If it's the kind of exam that determines whether you get a place to study at Oxford or Harvard, then it's easy to make a case that the result influences the rest of your entire life. But even if the stakes are much lower, there's still the small matter of personal pride. No-one really wants to do badly in an exam, even if their motivation for learning was simply the learning itself – the exam still matters because we want to give a good account of ourselves. This is exactly the type of situation that riles the lizard inside your head.

Allow me to explain. The amygdala is a tiny part of your brain, part of the limbic system. It plays a crucial role in the survival of the human species and is responsible for the 'fight or flight' emotional responses that are particularly prevalent when we enter stressful situations like exams. It's often referred to as the lizard brain because while much of our brain has evolved more recently in evolutionary terms, the amygdala is the primitive part of our brain that we've had since early in our evolution as a species. It's the part of us that connects us to lizards and squirrels and chickens and other small animals – their brains don't have the logic, creativity and compassion that ours do, because their brains are *mostly* lizard brains. But despite the complexities of the human brain – and the ingenuity that means as a species we dominate the world's resources like no other animal – we still have our lizard brains to help us survive. The lizard brain's principle concerns are comfort, hunger, reproduction, safety, territory and survival; and because these things used to mean life or death, the lizard inside your head usually shouts louder than the more rational and logical parts of your brain, too.

The problem is, your lizard brain can misfire. So if you're doing work that's going to be judged by an examiner, by your tutors, by your peers, by your family, or even just by yourself, your lizard brain is likely freaking out. He's screaming in your ear, 'don't do this, it's risky', or, 'I've not done enough work here, I'm going to get found out' (regardless, of course, of how much work you have or haven't done!), or, 'all my friends seem to know more than I do' (again, disregarding evidence) or, 'people will laugh at me'. And so on and so on. As I write this, I'm coming to the end of the process of writing this book, a time that I know from experience that the lizard brain hates – and will kick into gear vociferously. The lizard brain would rather that I don't put books out into the world, because he's worried that they might receive negative reviews which in turn might mean professional ruin (again, ignoring the rational fact that they might also receive good reviews and mean success). So much of how we view risk – in life, in work, in family situations, financially – is driven not by our rational mind but by our lizard brain. If someone is innately cautious it's probably because they have a loud lizard. If someone takes huge risks, it's probably because they have a loud lizard they've learned to ignore. And either way, your lizard is the cause of so much procrastination, worry, self-sabotage and stress.

Your lizard wants to ensure that you stay part of 'the pack', so wants you to fit in and do everything in the most conventional and boring ways possible because that's the safest way to survive. He hates conflict, he wants you to blend in, not stand out, he gets jealous at the drop of a hat and is extremely territorial (yep, those moments you feel livid that someone is jumping in front of you in a queue when in hindsight it didn't matter that much – that's him too!).

Unfortunately, you can't get rid of the lizard brain, or even shut it up – after all your lizard brain is rightly there for the rare situations where we are confronted with something that really is a matter of life and death, and he's just doing his job – but you can learn to recognize his pernicious little voice as something separate from your rational self. Then, you can start to adopt tactics to overpower him, so that you can get more work done, reduce your stress and feel better about your decisions.

LIZARD BRAIN EXAM THOUGHTS
Here are some of the ways you'll act if your lizard brain is pleading for you to stay away from exam halls, and indeed anywhere that he feels threatened:

▶ Burying your head in the sand (or a movie!) instead of revising for the exam.

▶ Telling yourself and others: 'I don't even want to *think* about the exam.'

▶ Imagining every possible worst-case scenario if you fail the exam or get a low mark.

▶ Playing these scenarios out to hideous conclusions, where you end up directionless, jobless, loveless and penniless.

▶ Eating instead of studying.

▶ Doing anything instead of facing the conversation with yourself about your revision plan and what to do next.

▶ Tidying your room or your desk instead of facing the work.

▶ Saying: 'I'll just do [insert random activity] to "warm up" before I start revising.'

▶ Feeling on edge with pre-exam nerves.

▶ Listening to everyone else's accounts after the exam of how they think they did (remember that you don't know if their own lizard brains are shouting loudly, or whether they're fighting their lizard brain by boasting to save face – and you can't do anything about it now anyway!).

▶ Being jealous of other people who seem to be 'cleverer' or find exams 'easy'.

None of these are rational. Think about it. Apply a moment's rational thought to each of them and you'll either laugh at them, or cry at how much credence and time you've given your evil little lizard in the past. And like I said, you'll be living with your lizard until the day you die, so the trick here is to recognize these thoughts so that you can challenge them. What unites most of them is fear, so one thing you can do is to create a bigger fear so that the lizard is suddenly on your side instead of thrashing against you.

SCARE YOUR LIZARD

Here's what often happens if you procrastinate over writing an essay or assignment. Your lizard brain shouts loudly that you're not pre-pared, that it'll be boring, that it'll get a low mark, that your choice of topic is silly, that you'll be ridiculed. So you're stuck. You can't write, you can't start, you can even feel like there's a magnetic force field repelling you from your desk.

Yet what happens a couple of days (or a few hours!) before the dead-line? Suddenly you realize that you can't stay in denial forever. You realize that you really do have to deliver something before that dead-line, that there are real people drumming their fingers on a desk somewhere, waiting for your work. And miraculously, you start. You don't just start, but you work like a workhorse, ignoring the lizard, ignoring *everything* in fact. You find a Zen-like Calm in the middle of the storm, where the only thing that matters in the world for those few hours or days is the thing you're working on – and you push on through.

So what is really happening here? The lizard is motivated by fear and wants to fit in. As you procrastinate, his fear is that you'll produce bad work, stand out and be ridiculed. Then, as the deadline approaches, he is still fearful, but the fear has changed. Now, the biggest risk becomes the risk of letting down the person who you're supposed to deliver the work to, or admitting to your tutor or someone you love that you've missed the deadline. So your lizard is suddenly on your side. Instead of, 'No! Don't do this!', he's yelling, 'Quick! Do this!' No-one said he was rational, after all.

How can you scare your lizard with a bigger fear? Well, one way to do this is to replicate that scenario by creating some form of accountability. Hence, leaving exam revision until the last minute is much easier if the only consequence up until that point is that we'll let ourselves down (because the lizard doesn't really care about that, he's in his safe place). But if you arrange to meet up and revise with friends, you don't want to let them down.

---

www.stickk.com

Stickk is a website designed to help you create accountability. It works by helping you set goals, which you register with the site. Then, you can appoint a 'referee' (someone you know) who will hold you accountable. And here's the really cool part. You can also put some real cash on the line.

You can make bets with friends or family that you're actually going to do what you said you'd do, at the right time. And if you lose, they win. You can also nominate an 'anti-charity'. For example, imagine if someone said to you: 'OK, if you don't do your fifteen hours of exam revision by Sunday at 10pm, you have to give £50 to help cosmetics companies test more of their products on animals.' You can put real money on the line, and if you don't deliver, you'd hate the idea that the people or causes that you hate more than anything in the world are benefiting. Now that's a bigger fear. Game on.

CHEAT YOUR LIZARD

So that's how to scare your lizard into action. It's a great strategy, but it's high-octane, high stakes and possibly even enough to get the adrenaline flowing, so it's not an approach you should adopt with every single thing you're working on or you'll burn out. Another way to overpower the lizard is to cheat him. Create for him the illusion that everything is OK, and then when his back is turned, or he's asleep, jump with both feet into whatever it is you think he might resist. Great examples of this include blindly saying 'yes' to the things that you fear. Don't sleep on it, say yes right now, in front of people. Do it while you're just sat having a beer or a meal. I did this with the London Marathon a couple of years ago. I had been intrigued at the prospect of running a marathon, but I knew my lizard brain would procrastinate and go into avoidance mode, so at a dinner for a charity I'm on the board for, I boldly, without really thinking, said: 'Yes! I'll definitely run the marathon for you next year! Count me in.' My lizard woke me up the following morning saying, 'Oh no, what have you done?', but by then, he was resigned to me training and running the marathon, which I did.

The other thing about the lizard brain, which works for any kind of stress, is that if you convince your body that you're not stressed, you can actually reduce your stress. Think about how the body reacts to stress: your breathing becomes shallower, you hunch over instead of standing tall, you might even stare at the floor. If, instead, you can stand tall, smile, breathe deeply and embody someone who has no fear, it will actually reduce the level of fear-chemicals in your brain. This is often referred to as creating a 'state'. Giving yourself some positive signals to jump on can often be enough to quieten your lizard.

RIDICULE YOUR LIZARD

Finally, let your lizard air his views, and then ridicule the hell out of him! There are many ways to do this. Meditation and mindfulness techniques, which we discussed earlier in the book, are partly designed to do this. They allow you to notice and observe your thought processes and gain an understanding of what's really going
on in your mind. There are many other ways, too. In Julia Cameron's book *The Artist's Way*, she describes a process called 'Morning Pages'. Basically, it involves waking up in the morning and soon afterwards, free-writing three full pages of your notepad. You write down whatever strange, idiotic or crazy thoughts are in your mind. It's a cathartic process, partly because once you've finished writing three pages, you can tear them out of the pad and throw them in the rubbish bin. But what you've done in that moment is allow the lizard to blurt out all that nonsense. Seeing the lizard's ridiculousness right there on the page is often enough for you to laugh in his silly little face. So once you get to know your lizard, you'll hear his screams above your rational thoughts and you can slap such idiocy down.

BEFORE EXAMS: NINJA PREPAREDNESS

The mindset of Ninja Preparedness means reassuring yourself (and your lizard) that you're well-placed to deal with whatever comes your way. Of course part of this is about whether you've done your revision and memorized the right things, but part of it too is identifying the things you can do before the exam to make it go more smoothly:

IT'S ONLY YOUR ROUTINE THAT MATTERS

Don't get carried away worrying about everyone else's routines. You may be more of a night owl or more of a morning person, you may have had highs and lows, but don't let anyone convince you their preparation has been perfect. Do things your own way.

LEAVE STUFF FRESH IN YOUR MIND

Just before you enter the exam hall, you can use the recency effect to your advantage. Take the most important bits of information or reading with you, and read those just before you're called in. Hopefully by this moment, you're only recapping (!), but if you want to leave a few things fresh in your mind, this is a great trick.

LAST-MINUTE REVISION SHOULD USE YOUR ADRENALINE

As we mentioned in the last chapter, cramming the night before is not a good idea. Make sure you've had a good night's sleep instead. It can be difficult to close the books and go to bed if you don't feel prepared yet, but seriously, the sleep is the preparation you need right now! Then, when you wake up on the morning of the exam, you'll feel the adrenaline kicking in. A great thing about this adrenaline is that it sends your brain into hyper-absorption mode. So take deep breaths and recap your revision for an hour or so before you head to the exam hall.

WALK BEFORE THE EXAM

Warm up your brain with a twenty-minute walk before the exam. This is a great time for some last-minute glances of your notes as you walk along and warm up, but also a great opportunity to listen to your lizard brain, calm yourself down and get into the Ninja Focus zone, too. Make sure you do both!

DEVELOP AN EXAM CHECKLIST

The easiest way to prepare for exams is to create a simple checklist. On the checklist you list the things you need to take with you ('1. Clear plastic bag, 2. Three pens for writing, 3. My student ID, 4. My scientific calculator', and so on). This checklist can be created at any time, but preferably on a day when you're not stressed – perhaps as the ultimate piece of 'Productive Procrastination'! Then, once it's done, it means you don't need to think too much about practicalities the night before, and you can relax and concentrate on getting a good night's sleep.

EAT A SLOW-RELEASE BREAKFAST

Make sure your brain is as fuelled-up as possible. Skipping breakfast on an exam day is a terrible error, which has been found to reduce thinking skills by up to 40%. What you're trying to achieve here is a slow release of energy throughout the morning or day. To boil down the whole subject of nutrition to no more than a couple of lines, you should concentrate on two rules: 1. More protein, less sugar. 2. Low Glycemic Index foods (GI). So things like salmon and eggs (perhaps an omelette with added vegetables like spinach and tomatoes) are great for giving the brain lots of protein, which aids your thinking. Likewise, things like wholegrain breads, muesli and porridge are 'low-GI' foods, which avoid sugar highs and make sure you get a 'drip drip' of energy all day. Lots of cereals – even the healthy-looking ones – are packed full of refined sugars, so are not ideal (but still better than nothing). Likewise, excessive amounts of fruit juice can seem like a great healthy option, but even the natural sugars in fruit will give you a sugar rush from which you'll crash later. Equipping the body with brain fuel foods will also help lower your stress and help you feel prepared. Getting Weapon-savvy with your food is a wise Ninja move – and try if possible to get into good habits before exam day, so that on the day itself you're not eating or preparing anything new.

REMEMBER: PRACTISE EXAM PERFORMANCE ITSELF, NOT JUST NOTE-TAKING

Finally in this section, there's no excuse in the age of Google for arriving at an exam having not practised *exams* on a regular basis. Even if your own course doesn't offer past papers (or access is limited) you can access past papers for your subject from institutions around the country or around the world. To find these easily on Google, type in 'site:ac.uk [subject] exam' if you're in the UK – other countries have their own domain name suffixes (if you're in the USA, type in 'site:edu', for example). And in the square brackets, write the name of the subject or even the particular topic you want to test yourself on. This should open up a whole load more past papers than you had access to before.

PRACTICAL STUFF: DURING THE EXAM

When the day comes, if your nerves are jangling it can be difficult to stay calm and maintain top-level performance. Here are a few techniques that should help you give the best account of yourself possible in any exam:

DON'T WRITE ANYTHING FOR THE FIRST TEN MINUTES

When you arrive at the exam, there's that tense moment where you turn over the paper and glance over the questions at a hundred miles an hour. It's a heightened moment of truth, where you're either surprised, relieved or terrified. It can be tempting at this point to dive right in, as you feel like you want to respond to the questions at the same hundred-mile-an-hour speed. Do the opposite.

Spend the first ten minutes of the exam reading and re-reading the questions. Spend some time looking at the available marks for each question and continue to resist the temptation to start writing. Make some notes about any 'no-brainer' decisions for questions you definitely want to tackle, but also keep an open mind and don't jump to any final conclu-sions just yet. Take your time, make sure you really understand not just the questions, but how you might answer each of them. You might see a topic that's fresh in your mind, but on closer inspection, the question itself might be a stinker and only worth a small number of marks.

Then, before you start, map out your timings from beginning to end, leaving a margin of around fifteen minutes at the end for tidying up, checking your paper and reviewing your work (of course this time may get eaten into, but it's better to have something to eat into than to run out of time). Also, as you plan, a good tip is to 'front-load' the first half of the exam (i.e. aim to get more than half done in the first half of the exam). That's because you'll be fresher in the first half, and you're going to tackle the easiest questions first.

START WITH THE EASY STUFF

While this might seem counterintuitive from an attention management point of view, getting an 'easy' question out of the way early will calm the nerves and hopefully should mean that you get a little ahead of yourself in terms of your timings (see above). Aim to answer the questions fully, but quickly, and give yourself the gift of some added time for the harder questions.

EQUATE TIME TO MARKS

In an exam, your time available and the marks available should be linked currencies. If it's a 90-minute exam and there are 60 marks, that means you've got one and a half minutes to get each mark. And if there are three questions of twenty marks each, take half an hour for each. Make sure you write this down fully as part of your planning – it's easy to glance at this but get it wrong in the heat of the moment. Most courses will let you know how many questions there will be before the exam, so if possible, work these timings out beforehand.

DON'T BE AFRAID TO DOODLE

Use a page on the question paper or some scrap paper to do mind maps, sketches and outlines. Getting your thinking out onto paper is a productive habit in every other setting in life, so why not do the same in the exam room?

USE CAFFEINE SPARINGLY AND STRATEGICALLY

For the same reasons that it's important to have a good, low-GI breakfast, it's important to avoid overusing coffee, energy drinks or any other drinks full of sugar and caffeine. Remember, we're looking for a slow and consistent release of energy to the brain, not the roller-coaster ride that caffeine offers. The occasional coffee to give you a little pep is OK, especially if strategically timed for long exams, but energy drinks should really be renamed 'spike-and-fall-flat drinks' and are best avoided.

GO FOR A WEE

Again, this seems counterintuitive, but if it's allowed, go to the loo in the middle of the exam. Plan to do this, before you even start. Why? Because this will encourage you to stay hydrated and drink water, and walking to the loo will temporarily raise your heart rate and increase your concentration. It will also give you a chance to get some perspective and think about things differently. Most tutors will say things like, 'if you reeeeally need to go, here's the plan …' and talk about leaving the exam room as some kind of criminal offence (or at least criminal waste of exam time), but of course you're using the break intentionally as a way to think about things differently, so don't treat it as dead time, treat it as a re-boot for your brain.

WALK TALL

To deal with the nerves of an exam, trick your lizard brain (and everyone else in the room) by displaying the body language of a champion. Walk tall, sit up straight, smile, relax the muscles in your face and shoulders, relax your jaw and tongue … As you

bring awareness to your body, you'll send calming signals back up to the brain which will in turn calm you down.

BREATHE DEEPLY
Stress is also exacerbated by short, hyper-ventilating breaths. Breathing slowly and deeply from the chest is another way to induce calm.

DON'T LOOK FOR PATTERNS IN MULTIPLE CHOICE
Being the person who sets the exam questions is a tedious job. Being the person who marks the exam questions or even compiles the marks is a tedious job. And if you do either or both of those jobs for a long time, it makes you either devious or bitter. So one way to take some revenge might be to set 25 multiple choice questions and make all the answers 'a'. As an examiner you're doing two things here. Firstly, you're daring the students who know the answers to put faith in their own knowledge. Secondly, you're reducing the possibility of flunky and flaky students getting decent grades because if you know half the answers are 'a', you would probably quite naturally guess the ones you didn't know to be 'b', 'c' or 'd'. So treat each and every question on its merits. Avoid doing what the brain will do naturally, which is to look for patterns. There are no patterns, just questions and answers.

AFTER THE EXAM

After the exam finishes, there's only one thing to do – get out of there as quickly as possible. Adopting Ninja Stealth and Camouflage at this moment will save you a lot of hassle with your lizard brain. If you have other exams to come in the days ahead, you don't need to be hearing everyone else's accounts of how they felt the exam went. Your fate – good or bad – is already sealed, and speculation by your lizard brain will only serve to create stress. Once the exam is gone, it's gone, so move onto the next one as quickly as possible. And if it's your last exam, advance quickly to the end-of-exams party before your lizard brain has any chance to chip in and ruin your next few weeks while you wait for the results.

Ninja Cheats

▶ Breathe. So much of your brain's performance is hindered by the nerves, adrenaline and panic of exam rooms. If you do nothing else, remember to breathe deeply, supplying more oxygen to the brain.

▶ Get over your exam anxieties, because they're not yours, they belong to your inner lizard. To find out more about him and how you can shut him up, go to page 244.

▶ Focus on you – the calmer you are, the more you'll remember and the more confidence you'll have to stay rational and focussed.

Are you a Study Ninja?

▶ A Study Ninja uses Mindfulness to stay aware of their worries and manage their emotions (keeping that pesky lizard in check).

▶ A Study Ninja is Ruthless in their pursuit of peak performance.

▶ A Study Ninja is Prepared, realizing that the hours of day-to-day magic that they've put in all year long will ultimately pay off in the exam room.

9.
PROCRASTINATION
UNDERSTANDING IT, STARTING AND KEEPING THE MOMENTUM GOING

THE SCIENCE OF PROCRASTINATION

The Oxford Dictionary definition of procrastination is 'to defer action, especially without good reason', while an academic study by Rothblum, Solomon and Murakami defined procrastination as 'the tendency to a) always or nearly always put off academic tasks and b) always or nearly always experience problematic anxiety associated with this procrastination'.

The word 'procrastination' has its origins in Latin, combining the words 'pro', meaning 'forward' or 'in favour of' and 'crastinus', meaning 'of tomorrow'. But while you might think humans have been procrastinating since the beginning of time, scientific study of the phenomenon is pretty patchy up until the late 20th century. One of the most famous studies often cited is Ringenbach's 1971 book on the subject. (This is, in fact, an elaborate academic in-joke: the book doesn't exist as the author never got around to writing it.)

In 2007, Piers Steel from the University of Calgary did conduct a meta-analysis of the topic, and his findings show just how big a problem procrastination really is for students. It's estimated that 80–90% of college students engage in procrastination, while 75% consider themselves procrastinators and 50% said they procrastinated 'consistently and problematically'. Students reported that procrastination took up over a third of their daily activities, often including in this sleeping, socializing or watching TV. And all the studies point to it being an issue on the rise.

A 2004 study by the Gail Kasper Consulting Group (USA) found that students are not the only ones to feel guilty. Just under three weeks before the deadline, 29% of people had yet to file their taxes with the US Government. The top two reasons they gave for delay? Fear of owing the government money and 'poor time management skills'. Similar studies have also found that Americans made $473 million of overpayments, due to making last-minute errors or not having time to check their figures. So it seems government revenues might be the only winner when it comes to procrastination.

There are plenty of losers, though. Dianne Tice and Roy Baumeister's 1997 study in the journal *Psychological Science* rated college students on an established scale of procrastination, then tracked their academic performance, stress and general health throughout a semester. Initially there actually seemed to be a benefit to procrastination, as the students who were higher procrastinators had lower levels of stress compared to others – although this is probably a result of them engaging in more fun activities while everyone else was getting down to some serious work. But as the semester rolled on, the problems mounted up for the procrastinators. They earned lower grades than other students and reported higher cumulative amounts of stress and illness. Tice and Baumeister concluded that: 'Procrastinators end up suffering more and performing worse than other people.'

Three years later, Tice and Ferrari did another experiment where they brought students into a laboratory and told them that at the end of the session they'd be engaging in a maths puzzle. Some were told the task was a meaningful test of their cognitive abilities, while others were told that it was just designed to be meaningless fun at the end. Before doing the puzzle, the students had a period of time in which they could either prepare for the puzzle, or just wait and mess around with games like Tetris. Chronic procrastinators only avoided preparing for the puzzle when they were told it was a meaningful test – the procrastinators that were told it was just meaningless fun behaved no differently from non-procrastinators. Of course, we know that our lizard brain hates the idea of being judged or tested, and what we learn here is just how self-defeating our own minds can really be.

Academic studies into procrastination list a wide range of causes, including cognitive distortions, genetics, personality types and demographics, as well as thought patterns and traits like perfectionism, conscientiousness, neuroticism, low self-esteem and fear of failure. What's clear is that it's a mixture of nature and nurture. Personally, I find this a very comforting thought: some of us are more prone to procrastination than others, and we should acknowledge that this is just part of what makes us human. And yet part of our procrastination is also within our power to change – we will never shut up that lizard brain completely, but we can do lots to make sure he doesn't get in our way quite so often.

When I coach people in productivity, a desire to reduce procrastination manifests in two wishes that people have: 'I need to know how to get started' and 'I need to know how to keep going.' So we're getting deep-down and practical in this chapter, with twenty strategies for getting started and then five ways to keep things going.

Before we get into it, a few words about how to use this chapter. All of what you'll find below is, in some way, a trick of the mind. This is because we're fighting fire with fire. Procrastination is an evil trick of the mind (specifically, our lizard brain) and the way to defeat it is with tricks of the mind, too. Your mind is different from mine and from that of everyone you  know, so don't expect all of these strategies to work for you straight away, and don't worry about this, either – you don't need them all. In fact, you might just find one thing that works like a treat for a long time, and then one day it might stop working, as the lizard gets wise to your approaches and develops new ways to throw you off track, and you'll need to try something else. Different things might work at different times of the year or with different types of task, too. So think of the below as a kind of toolbox: try the wrench, and if that doesn't work, try clubbing yourself on the head with a spanner instead.

20 STRATEGIES FOR GETTING STARTED

1. **Microgoals**

Writing an essay or working on something big can seem frustrating. This is because the brain releases a chemical called dopamine into the brain when we complete things. In fact, dopamine is often known as the reward molecule. Its function in evolutionary terms was to make sure that we found happiness and value in hunting food *before* we were hungry in case, when we did get hungry, no food was available to kill. And the reason we've evolved and survived as a species? Dopamine is highly addictive. Ever written something on your to-do list just for the pure pleasure of crossing it out? Ever got obsessed with completing something that you could have left until later (whether it's putting food in your kitchen cupboard or answering an email)? These are our quests for dopamine. When we don't get to experience that regular sense of completion, we don't get our dopamine fix, so the trick is to break what you're working on down into microgoals.

A microgoal with a 2,000 word essay might be to do 250 words a day. Guess what? If that's your microgoal and you hit it, you'll feel good about having done 250 words and won't be feeling bad that you haven't yet done the other 1,750. And if you hit your microgoal every day for a week and a day, you've finished your essay without even realizing it. Anything you're working on can be broken down into microgoals, but there are a few things to bear in mind:

▶ A microgoal only works if you trust you'll continue working on it (so be mindful of your schedule in the coming days).

▶ A microgoal needs to be specific and measurable.

▶ Remember the 'Planning Fallacy': things generally take longer than we estimate. While working in microgoals can help to reduce the effect of the Planning Fallacy, you will still underestimate how long things take, so make sure you also leave some extra time for this.

If in doubt, break it down into smaller, measurable chunks and give yourself something more manageable to point your efforts at.

2. Go dark

A recent study found that for every one-minute email interruption, it takes on average fifteen minutes to recover and get back onto the thing you were doing. So all those little tiny distractions add up to a huge inefficiency.

Sometimes what you're doing needs total focus. For these times, go dark. 'Going dark' is a phrase that is thought to have originated among software developers in the days before a big deadline. When they're working away on something that requires total focus, they disappear off the radar. They're not answering their phones or emails and you don't know where they are in the office (assuming they're even *in* the office at all). I use this tactic regularly, because I think there are certain tasks where I'm very prone to procrastination if I don't have total focus, but actually once I do focus, it becomes really clear what I need to do and how to get started. I tend to spend my mornings in my home office, and I'll often turn off my home internet connection and make sure my phone is on silent, or leave it in another room.

For a couple of hours I can get lost in what I'm doing, and the results of this can be tremendous. For the same reason, when I'm writing books I tend to close down my Facebook account and set my email to 'Out of Office' for a few weeks. The problem with 21st-century connectivity is it creates an obligation to connect – and the inconvenient truth is that much of our best work happens when we're not connected. There's fun, magic and ridiculous creativity to be found in the art of Ninja Stealth and Camouflage. Don't apologize for occasionally being unavailable – in fact, promote it as fundamental for yourself and others.

3. Avoid the blank page, don't avoid the blank page

One of the hardest things about getting started is staring at a blank page. So much so that it almost repels you from sitting down to start. We avoid even the thought of staring at the blank page because it feels daunting, and the infinite possibility of it feels somehow threatening. 'How can I possibly turn this into something valuable?', we think. Well, you know what? Every book you've read started with a blank page. *Star Wars* was once a blank page. Your favourite album of all time was once a blank page. Everything invented was once a blank page. But you know how each and every one of those things got good? They got good because the first draft was shitty. The ideas evolved, they didn't just arrive in perfect form.

So just write something. Start something. *Anything!* It doesn't matter for now what it is, how good it is, whether you end up ditching it or using it. It's just that sometimes, having something to disagree with is the first step to knowing what you want to do. And seeing some words on the page gives you something to do, rather than staring into the infinite abyss of a page of white nothingness.

4. One Pomodoro

We talked about the Pomodoro Technique back in chapter five. So grab a kitchen timer, or a Pomodoro app on your phone, and just do the first 25 minutes of the thing that's scaring you. You don't need to finish it, it's not important how far you get, but just start it. I often use this technique with things that I find mind-numbingly boring, like filling in excel spreadsheets about finances. What I find is that one Pomodoro is always enough to turn my discomfort with a task into something more comfortable. And the thought of just spending 25 minutes on something rather than feeling trapped and hemmed in by the idea of spending the whole morning on it makes it easier for me to get going. At the end of one Pomodoro, I'm usually happy to carry on until the thing is finished, so it's a great way of tricking myself into getting going. You don't even need to do 25 minutes, either. You could use this same tip but just change it to doing 'the first five'. Often, five minutes and the act of starting will be enough to create some momentum and help you get over your fear.

5. Take your lizard for a walk

OK, so let's say you've established that you don't have a procrastination problem, you have a lizard brain problem. Your lizard is scared, he thinks your reputation is on the line, your entire future is on the line, your family's view of you is on the line and even your self-esteem is on the line. These are very real concerns to have, it's just that your lizard lives in a fantasy land that exaggerates all the failures (and possible failures) while ignoring all of the successes. But your logical mind is right to be concerned about your future and your reputation. So listen to that lizard. Don't try to ignore him today, but argue with him instead.

You can take your lizard for a walk by letting him run riot on a notebook page. Write down how he's feeling and everything he's screaming at you. Seeing those words on the page will help you work out what's real and what's exaggerated nonsense (I think you can guess what you'll find, but it really helps when you see it written down). Alternatively, take your lizard for a real walk. Living by the sea, I always take my lizard to the beach. For me, there's something wonderful about my lizard brain seeing the sea because he sees how insignificant everything is – 'I'm just a freaked-out part of a brain of some guy walking along a beach on a tiny island in the middle of a tiny planet …' And at the same time, my logical mind sees the sea differently. It sees possibility, Christopher Columbus setting sail, the land that might be on the other side of that sea, all that good stuff.

And what's funny is that, like a small dog, after a couple of hours of walking, your lizard gets really tired. His resistance to what you want to do often ebbs away once you've take him for a little walk.

6. **Overpromise. (Sometimes.)**

Generally, overpromising on things is a terrible and destructive habit. We all need to be clear about our goals and stop trying to please people by agreeing to things that don't fit into what we're trying to achieve. It can be all too easy to say yes to lots of things that don't matter and even easier to overpromise how much you can deliver in a short timescale.

But there's a time when overpromising can actually be one of the greatest productivity weapons you have – and that time is when you're procrastinating and need the accountability of having something to prove. Saying yes, against your better judgement, throwing down a challenge to yourself to get something done on a ridiculously tight timescale can be thrilling and exciting. The power of the deadline or expectation it creates can get you over the start line and hurtling towards completion with momentum that goes off the usual scale. It forces you to commit, forces you to follow through and in turn, forces you to say no to lots of other things that will come your way, as you manage the monster you have created.

This isn't for the faint of heart and shouldn't be a trick you practise regularly, but a little bit of exhilaration and the occasional late night are fine; I'd argue that they're part of life's rich tapestry of experiences and are to be celebrated. Just be careful not to make this a regular part of your routine. When the occasional crunches become constant exhaustion and eventual burnout then it's as far from thrilling as can be.

7. **Turn 'I don't know' into 'what if I did know?'**

The language we use with ourselves determines what we think about things. We convince ourselves that we don't know where to start. We convince ourselves that we don't know what to do. We convince ourselves that we don't know anything at all. And yet this is never true. We always know where to start, even if the place we should start is to ask someone else's advice, or flesh out what it is we're stuck on.

Being stuck and not knowing are two very different things. We confuse them regularly, but deep down, we always know. So next time you get into an inner-narrative that goes something like this …

'Where should I start? Ohhh, I don't know …'

… continue this conversation by adding a new question: 'But what if I did know? What would the answer be then?' What if you really did know what to do? What would that 'doing' look like? Make it hypothetical for a moment if that helps you. Imagine what *someone else* would be doing if *they* knew the answer. Then start with that.

8. Mindfulness and DUST

Why can't you muster up some Ninja Focus? Maybe it's because you haven't worked out what the problem with starting really is. What is it that you're actually resisting? Back to our friend the DUST model for procrastination. Is it Difficult? If so, what kind of help you need becomes a good next question: do you need some research or some advice to help you? Is it because the work is Undefined? Have you worked out what the project is really about, what the end-point will look like, how to judge success, and what the first actions to take need to be?

Is what you're working on Scary? Are you worried about the consequences and need some reassurance? Do you need to take that lizard brain for a walk to put how scary it is in perspective? Perhaps it's just something Tedious – a task that the Lazy, Scatterbrained version of you just can't be bothered to start. Those YouTube videos are way more entertaining, after all.

Sometimes, thinking about the DUST model, and noticing what's behind our thoughts and behaviours is enough to diagnose the problem and unstick things. If you're wandering around in a fug and not allowing your procrastination thoughts to come to the surface, it's difficult to solve the problem.

This is where mindfulness techniques like meditation or free-writing can help. By paying enough attention to whatever it is that's diverting your attention, you create the diagnosis – and from there it's so much easier to find the cure.

9. Productive Procrastination

Here's a Ninja secret. Sometimes it's OK to procrastinate … because other things get done! Procrastinating by tidying your room, or cooking a massive chilli con carne to feed you for a week, or sorting out all your revision notes or even by going to bed early to get enough sleep so that you'll feel fresher tomorrow aren't the worst things you can do. Much worse than any of these things is procrastinating with activities that contribute nothing to your sense of achievement or Balance. Sometimes it's worth throwing in the towel for the day, admitting defeat and finding something else vaguely useful to do. Being kind to yourself on a day like this will pay dividends the following day.

When I'm writing a book, it's amazing how clear my email inbox is. My logic is that if I'm avoiding writing, the least I should do is avoid it by hiding somewhere worthwhile, so I answer all my emails. It's amazing how much being scared of a bigger thing motivates you to do other things that were themselves previously too scary, or just boring or difficult. What if I told you your procrastination can be a productivity weapon to everything else in the world, as well as a barrier to the one thing you're procrastinating about? Suddenly it doesn't seem so bad, does it?

This brings us back to the fact that a Study Ninja is a human, not a superhero. Even with all the techniques in this book, you'll never create perfect habits that never let you down. And you shouldn't try. Recognize that we all have off days. It's part of life. What matters is what you do when those things come along, and as long as the answer isn't 'continue beating myself up for hours on end' then something good will come of it. Choose Productive Procrastination over the more pernicious type.

10. **Dopamine rushes**

Linked to this is the idea of chasing dopamine rushes. The brain feeds you dopamine whether you're tidying your desk or tackling an assignment, so when we're Productively Procrastinating, we're often just chasing the next little 'hit' of dopamine. And it is highly addictive – it's also the chemical linked to alcohol abuse, gambling and a whole slew of other addictive behaviours. So set up a little string of dopamine rushes to strive for. The first could be completing tidying your desk, the second could be filling out that annoying bank form you've been putting off, and then the third one could be drafting the outline for the essay.

Before, it was the essay you were avoiding, but now it's just the third hit of dopamine. And once you've chased down those other two, your brain will be hungry for more. Your brain will be tricked into seeing the scary task as being the same as those other more trivial ones once you're on a roll.

11. **Go weird**

Procrastination and the stress it brings can be crippling. It can produce such inactivity and stasis that it makes you feel 'stuck in a rut', unable to do anything to break free. Days can become monotonous and you can become detached from the passion and purpose of what you're doing and why you're doing it. Sometimes, when your usual techniques aren't shifting the blockage, you need to go weird. So if your usual routine isn't working, why not try waking at 4am instead, or napping all afternoon and then studying all night?

There are lots of ways to go weird with what you're working on. Try picking a word at random. And if that sounds like too much pressure (or if you want to make sure it's truly random) you can find a random word by opening a dictionary at a random page, clicking Google's 'I'm feeling lucky' button (without searching for anything) or picking a website like the BBC and choosing the 28th word on the first page you see. Now, see what you can do to incorporate that word into how you're working, or even what you're working on. So let's say the word that pops up is 'Chinese', then maybe take your laptop to a Chinese restaurant or go sit on a bench in Chinatown, or make a China plate your desk for the day. If the word is 'swimming', then try to get the acronym 'swim' into your revision notes to remember something important. Or sit and read in the local swimming pool cafe all day. Or sit at home wearing armbands as you do your work. If anyone asks you why you're doing this, remember that you don't need to justify your behaviour: 'What are those? Oh, nothing. I was procrastinating so I put on some armbands.'

This isn't as ridiculous as it sounds. A sense of playfulness can help reduce stress, and breaking with even the tiniest of conventions can help overcome the bigger barriers that you're trying to overcome.

12. Break down the task to the next physical action

In chapter two we talked about the idea of 'next physical actions' – how you can't actually 'do' a project, but you can turn the project into small, doable steps. We talked about how imagining where you're going to be when that thing gets done, and how visualizing it happening can help make your to-do list more palatable and manageable. Much of this is the battle between the Clever, Motivated you and the Lazy, Scatterbrained you. Even when you're a bit tired, you can do lots of the difficult things on your list, but only if you've already done the difficult thinking about where to start. So seeing 'email my tutor to ask her about my ideas for the assignment' on your to-do list promotes actions, whereas seeing 'assignment!!' provokes nothing but panic. Get into the mindset where you seek out 'next physical actions' as soon as you realize there's something you need to do, and turn the 'nags' that you write on paper as things you're worried about into things you can do something about.

And if you're stuck, go back and do this again. Have you fully identified, in clear language, what it is you need to do next? And no, 'get started with the assignment' isn't clear enough. 'Print out the notes' is clear enough, 'mind-map some ideas and structures' is clear enough, 're-read the text for half an hour' is clear enough. Be harsh with yourself here, until you're forcing yourself to actually identify a specific and physical next thing you can do.

13. Dancing to the right tune

Every time I hear certain music, I'm almost pre-programmed to get down to some serious work. Why? Because of something that psychologists call 'states'. You create a state of mind by doing something over and over again in the same kind of way. Subconsciously, my brain and my body both know that when they hear certain music, it's time to pay attention and get in the zone. Think Rocky training with 'Eye of the Tiger' blaring in the background, or how songs like 'Around the World' or 'One More Time' by Daft Punk make you want to jump around like a maniac or run for miles.

The one that really works for me is the album *Kind of Blue* by Miles Davis. What inspires me every time I put it on is the story of how it was made. It's a true masterpiece, but the whole thing was recorded in only seven hours of studio time. Of course it helps if you have genius ideas like Miles Davis, and that you've done all the preparation and rehearsal to bring together such a talented group of musicians. But it's possible to create a masterpiece in a day if you put your mind to it. That album is a constant reminder to me to get my Ninja Focus on.

And different kinds of music work better in different environments, too. If I want a couple of hours of hardcore Ninja Focus on a train or in a busy environment, it'll be something electronic and noisy, like a Matthew Herbert album or The Prodigy. And if I want creative ideas, I might listen to something really strange like Jimi Tenor or something that makes me feel very decadent and intellectual, like a Chopin piano concerto. What you might notice about all of those choices is that they're all for the most part instrumental styles of music, without too many words. I find that focussing any of my attention on the words of a song stops me from being able to create a 'state' from it, so I tend to find music that either has a few repetitive words or none at all. Actually, what you choose to listen to isn't really that important, as long as you're using the music to create the kind of 'state' you need. Once you start to feel the music pulling you to read more, or write more, or to sit at your desk and dream up ideas, you know you're on the right track.

14. Accountability: create a deadline in someone else's world

The carrot or the stick? It's far better to learn to create your own carrots (like microgoals, for example) and be self-motivated, than to need to constantly rely on the prospect of stick punishments to motivate you into action. But there are times when the stick has its place. We talked in the last chapter about accountability and why websites like stickk.com can create the ultimate in harsh motivation.

Lots of websites or books that talk about beating procrastination will mention setting your own internal deadlines. I think this is a load of nonsense. A deadline is only a deadline if you'll be dead if you don't get over the line. And if the person monitoring you to meet the deadline is you, then you'll secretly know that if you don't meet the deadline, nothing will happen. Far better to create a deadline in someone else's world. Having someone else depending on you delivering something at the right time – whether that's your tutor, a family member, or someone else on your course – is the only way to make a deadline an effective tool.

15. Be in awe of a 'first-world problem'

Do you know how *lucky* you are to be procrastinating?! Let's deconstruct this for a minute. You are sitting on the best planet we know of, in an amazing moment in the history of time. You are a human. That alone means you are *out* of the food chain. Most other animals don't have the time to procrastinate – they might get eaten! Then, you have shelter and enough food, and good odds too that you have a relatively stable environment and supportive relationships to help you as you learn. Isn't this amazing so far?!

But let's go on. You have the resources available to you to buy or read this book, to type into a computer, to buy yourself new study materials, new clothes whether you need them or not, new phones, new gadgets and so on. That's all pretty good, right? And now, ladies and gentlemen, I present to you … the internet!

You live in a time where *anything* you want to find out or see or know – anything! – is right there at your fingertips. Want to play a game for an hour? Sure. Care for some sushi, sir? Get it ordered! Want to buy a new watch at 3am? Step this way. Want to be able to get started with whatever book or film or music you've *just thought of,* that second? It's downloading for you as we speak, madam. Have any of us realized just how insanely lucky we are to be living in the internet age, and to be born onto part of the planet that is abundantly resourced with books and internet connections and personal disposable income to fritter away? The odds of this, as opposed to being born an amoeba or a gazelle, as opposed to having been born somewhere else at some other time, or not being born at all? It's a billion-to-one shot when you look at it that way. So really, we're so unbelievably lucky that one of our 'problems' is not being able to start a thing that's going to enrich our knowledge. And sometimes that's all the reminder I need to get over myself and get started. Life's a wonderful gift. Embrace it. What are you waiting for?

16. Anti-perfection

Perfection is a disease. A Study Ninja knows that too much emphasis on achieving perfection can leave us crippled by the prospect of failing to achieve it. But why do we obsess over perfection, anyway? There are of course times when perfect matters – if you're checking the plane's safety features or performing triple heart bypasses, then it's probably a good idea to aim for perfect. But most of the time, the aim should be 'good enough'. Once something is good enough, it's time to move on to the next thing.

I like to think that there's a certain glory in imperfection. A perfect world full of perfect things becomes boring – if every day in your life the weather is the same, then the weather doesn't really exist as a feature of your life. It's the 2% imperfection that gives the other 98% its character and value. And ultimately when we fail at things or things don't go perfectly, it's a reminder that we're human beings after all, and is a reminder of how remarkable that other 98% of our achievement really is. So seek out the Study Ninja's secret source of power – 'just enough' – right from the start. Never let yourself get obsessed with perfection and celebrate the rough edges.

17. Quantity takes care of quality

While we've discussed a lot of shortcuts in this book that really work (like speed-reading or using the 80-20 rule) there are lots more supposed shortcuts (like cramming) that are actually sub-optimal. Efficiency can take you a very long way, but after that there's no substitute for putting in the hours. Remember, as a learner, there's a direct relationship between the hours you put into studying and learning and what you get out of it. So your job as a Study Ninja is to make sure you show up. There may be days when you put the hours in, you're adopting everything in this book and you feel like a superhero. There may be days where the opposite is true. But ultimately, it's important to put the time in. Often when we procrastinate we avoid the hours because we're avoiding a decision or a starting point, but there are always new things you could explore, or Productive Procrastination opportunities you can find. So just because you're scared, doesn't mean you should stay in bed. Just because you don't know where to start on this thing, that shouldn't prohibit you from starting something. In the end, if you take care of the quantity by putting in the hours, your learning will take care of itself. If you're savvy with your strategies and approaches *and* put in the hours, then you're really onto something special.

18. Lower your expectations

One of the primary causes of stress is the weight of our own expectations. Procrastination is the gap between our intentions and our actions, so the bigger the gap, the more stress we're likely to feel. Lowering expectations – even temporarily – can help you to feel less guilty about the size of that gap and take the action you need to get started.

19. Practise 'behavioural chaining'

Psychologists talk about a technique called 'behavioural chaining', which can be very useful in developing momentum and beating procrastination. Basically, if you want to make an omelette, start by breaking an egg or chopping an onion. The act of doing this first part of the task means that before you even notice, you're underway. Similarly, if you want to paint the door of your bedroom, you're much more likely to do this if you've been out and bought paint. This is beating procrastination by becoming invested in something by having taken the first step. So if you want to revise or organize your notes, start by spreading your notes out over the desk. If you want to tidy your bedroom, do the classic thing of moving everything that needs to be tidied away onto the bed first. By suddenly feeling 'in' the task rather than worrying that you can't start it, you develop a different relationship with it, with fewer of the hang-ups.

20. The final throw of the dice

For a month in 2013, I made decisions by throwing dice as a substitute for procrastination and indecision. I chose what to eat, what to wear and I even wrote paragraphs of international contracts based on the decisions the dice gave me. Sometimes I used the dice to tell me yes or no (odds or evens), sometimes I came up with three options, and sometimes I allowed the throw to force me to think of six possibilities. I was doing this as part of a year of productivity experiments, working in strange and extreme ways to see what I could learn from it. The dice taught me some wonderful lessons. Firstly, when you're forced to think of six or even twelve possibilities, your mind moves away from the status quo pretty quickly, and you see a world ripe with possibility. Secondly, when you know that you have dice in your back pocket, you make a lot more decisions without needing them (slightly for fear of not wanting to turn to the dice). Thirdly, any decision is better than none, whether the dice arrived at it or you did – action of any kind trumps indecision. Fourthly, the dice liberate our ego. This is a strange one so bear with me. So many of our decisions are wrapped up in our own narratives. We might struggle with a decision because we're worried about making the wrong call and worried that we'll be blamed for the consequences. However, when you can surrender your control to the dice, it's exhilarating. Instead of feeling weighed down by the responsibility, you can blame the dice for the bad decisions and thank the dice for the good ones. And just experience whatever it is that comes along. The fifth and final lesson comes from an old Yorkshire saying that someone told me during my month of experimenting: 'You get a third of your decisions right, you get a third of them wrong, and the other third don't matter anyway.'

I'm not saying you should roll the dice to decide whether to attend your exam or not, but you could do worse things in a moment of procrastination than pull out some dice, come up with some options for what to do with the rest of that evening and enjoy the ride.

EXERCISE: LOOKING BACK, PLANNING AHEAD

Let's take a moment to reflect on procrastination and those twenty ways to get going again:

1. Can you identify some recent instances of your own procrastination?

2. What caused these instances? What do you think most worries

your lizard brain? Which of the techniques we've just talked about would be worth experimenting with?

3. It's often hard to predict, but what do you have coming up in your schedule that you think might lead to procrastination?

4. What will you try when that happens?

5. Do you have a regular way to reflect and remain mindful about your procrastination habits? (Perhaps some questions on your Weekly Checklist or something as part of a Daily Ritual?)

FIVE STRATEGIES FOR MAINTAINING MOMENTUM AND NINJA FOCUS

OK, so you've managed to break the impasse and get started. But what's to say that in an hour you won't be back where you started? Momentum is as easily lost as it is won, and a Study Ninja works on the self-control and self-motivation to maintain momentum for as long as possible. Here are five ways to keep yourself engaged and keep the show on the road:

1. The Power Hour

The Power Hour is an idea that I first introduced in *How to be a Productivity Ninja*. The idea is that doing the simple things consistently and well is the key to ongoing success. Think about your role as a student, or your roles outside of your learning, and ask yourself this question:

'What's the one activity that, if I did it consistently for an hour a day, every day this year, would make me successful?'

If you were a sales person, that activity might be cold calling. If you don't enjoy cold calling, you'll always find something else to do in its place. Developing a habit, though, that every day between 9.30 and 10.30am you cold-call will yield fantastic results over time. Every musician hates doing their scales practice, most sports people hate warming up. Depending on what you're studying, your Power Hour might be dedicated to reading, or language practice, or note-taking. Imagine you're being interviewed in a years' time and the interviewer is asking you: 'What do you attribute your brilliance to?' And imagine yourself answering: 'Well, it's pretty simple really. I just made sure that I set aside an hour a day for …'

Yes, brilliance comes in all shapes and sizes. Yes, surprising things will help you learn or help you achieve. But at the same time, doing the most obvious things consistently is one of those strategies that's so common sense it's almost painful, but so uncommonly practised it's insane.

EXERCISE: GETTING STARTED WITH THE POWER HOUR

OK, so let's schedule your very own Power Hour.

What time should it take place tomorrow? Will it be the same time every day?

The only two rules are:

1. Once you've committed to a Power Hour, you can't change the time or reschedule it (you wouldn't reschedule a meeting at short notice with your tutor, so why be more willing to let yourself down than you are to let down others?).

2. You can only have one Power Hour each day. The focus on consistently doing one thing well is what counts here.

An hour a day will give you astounding results. Your next job is to trust it and keep it going. Speaking of which ...

2. **Jerry Seinfeld's wall planner**

Jerry Seinfeld has been doing his own version of the Power Hour, and it's made him pretty successful! His secret to success is said to be a wall planner that he keeps in his house. It's one of those big ones where you can see the whole year mapped out. His aim is to make sure he writes every day and above all, that he doesn't 'break the chain'. What he does is marks each day that he writes with a red cross. Then, if he's written for ten consecutive days, he has a chain of ten red crosses. Even just thinking about this is making me want to write tomorrow, so that I have eleven! What I love about this simple piece of psychology is that once you're on a roll, your positive habits get stronger and stronger. You could use this to monitor your Power Hours, or use it to monitor a particular habit that you want to instil every day, like writing or background reading – just make sure you don't break that chain.

3. **Ninja Mindfulness and the art of regular review**

It's easy to see performing a Daily Review ritual, such as those we talked about in chapter two, as somehow superfluous. And sitting down with your Weekly Checklist to review each and every project and action on your plate right now? It's easy to start saying: 'I don't have time for that!' But the whole process of review is an investment. It's a way to reconnect with the bigger picture, with your higher purposes and aims, and be sure that what you're choosing to give your attention to are the right things.

So as well as providing that reassurance – which vitally means you can focus the rest of your time on the details and on *actually doing stuff*, rather than feeling constantly stressed about the big stuff – both daily and weekly review time promotes Mindfulness. Built into my checklists are a whole bunch of questions that help me to coach myself, steer myself towards correcting bad habits and of course, notice my own thoughts. If I'm feeling uneasy about a project, it's in the review times that I catch it first. If you're continuing to put off certain tasks, you might not even notice this if you don't engage with some form of review process, but spending those few minutes really thoroughly looking down my lists means there's nowhere for those tasks to hide – you very quickly develop a more intelligent awareness of your own strengths, weaknesses, preferences and power moves.

Never treat the opportunity for review as wasted time, see it as essential and sacred time. What you'll learn about yourself during those moments will make the rest of your days and weeks so much easier to manage, and you'll spend so much less time in a state of stress.

4. Other people

A Ninja doesn't like to feel that they're battling alone. Seeking the solace and support of others can really help to maintain momentum. There are some great examples of ways that you can come together as mini-communities, supporting each other in your learning. Just being around other motivated people can be a great motivator, and the energy becomes an infectious circle of achievement. Here are a few good examples of how getting together can bring the flow to what you're doing:

▶ **Writing groups.** I've heard of some phenomenal examples of PhD students who finished their entire (late-running) theses in 48 hours, because they were in a room surrounded by other people doing exactly the same. It doesn't have to be so extreme, but the idea of going to a place and being surrounded by everyone else in the same situation can be very inspiring.

▶ **Co-working spaces.** Ever wanted the buzz of an office but without all the office politics, or indeed, the job? Well you can sign up to be a member of a co-working space, where you'll be surrounded by all kinds of interesting and motivated people, creating businesses and changing the world. For a while when I lived in London, I worked out of a co-working space called Impact Hub (www.impacthub.net) and they have other hubs in cities all around the world. Many have their own etiquette and rules, one of which is that if you overhear a conversation on another table and have some way of helping that person's idea, it's not rude to butt in and talk to them about it. It makes it feel like you're sat working with a team of people, even though, of course, none of them are working on the same assignment as you.

▶ **Hack weekends.** Particularly popular in the tech community, the idea of hack weekends is to bring together groups of people to 'make something, start to finish' in 48 hours. You might be able to find hack communities or hack days where you can actually get people to make something that contributes to your learning (depending on your subject, of course), but even if you can't, going along and soaking up the energy can be a great motivator. I'm personally always inspired when I meet interesting people doing cool things. It inspires me that so many people are working to create a better bit of the world, and it always refocusses me to do the same.

5. **Momentum is always spiralling, never static**

Finally, I'm a big believer that ultimately, your momentum determines how far you can go. With procrastination, you're either stuck or you're not. It's a problem some of the time, but other times you don't need to give it a second thought. But I see momentum as a kind of spiral. You're either on an upward trajectory, or on a downward one that you need to reverse. Creating that initial burst of motivation to get over your procrastination hump can be difficult, so once you get going, don't settle for standing still or slowing down. The more momentum you create, the more effortless it becomes to create more. And the faster you're spiralling upwards, the higher you can go. For the same reason, when you see the momentum dipping slightly, don't wait until you come to a procrastination standstill again – do everything you can to reverse that downward spiral.

There's something really special about operating in a state of playful, productive momentum and relaxed control. As a Study Ninja, you now have all the weapons at your disposal to do exactly that. As you're probably finding already as you put this all into action, it's a far better way to live your life than muddling through – and there's something satisfying and freeing about winning your battles with the demons of temptation, workload and procrastination. So now that we've got this learning business well and truly sussed out, I want to leave you with one final thought.

EXERCISE: STOP, START, CONTINUE

We're reaching the end of the book here. I'm conscious that we've covered a lot of ground and that while you may have made some changes already, there will be plenty of new ideas buzzing around your head as you continue your quest for Study Ninja status. So let's take a moment to think about your habits – good and bad – and how to apply this book to your world.

Three questions:

1. What do you need to STOP doing, as a result of this book?

2. What three things are you going to START doing as a result of this book?

3. What do you do well already, that you're going to CONTINUE to do as a result of being reassured by this book?

Ninja Cheats

▶ Get beyond saying, 'I'm procrastinating', or ignoring the work. You need to work out what it is you're scared of. Use the DUST model on page 51 to think this through. Until you know this, it's difficult to overcome procrastination.

▶ Do something. Anything. Getting started is the hardest part. You don't need to read a book about it right now, you just need to START. So go on, put the book down and start – it's not as hard as you think.

▶ Don't focus on perfectshun.

Are you a Study Ninja?

▶ A Study Ninja uses Mindfulness to understand themselves, helping get to the heart of why they're procrastinating.

▶ A Study Ninja recognizes that they're Human, not Superhero, and that procrastination is a natural part of human nature.

▶ This in turn gives the Study Ninja a chance to exercise Balance – being kind to yourself when you're under pressure is important and often overlooked.

10. CURIOSITY AND CHILDISHNESS

NEVER MIND THE ANSWERS, HOW ABOUT ASKING BETTER QUESTIONS?

It's often said that the role of learning is to grow – that by acquiring knowledge we somehow grow up, grow old or grow wise. But I actually don't think this is true. When learning truly excites us, we might grow as a person, but actually we don't grow up, old or wise. The more we learn, the more we become curious, childlike, and questing of mind, as we seek answers and begin to seek yet more questions.

We don't grow old, because the excitement and wonder of the world stops us doing so. We feel like a child on an adventure, in awe of everything around us and wanting to absorb as much of it as we can, as quickly as we can. There's a sense of urgency that defies the ageing process somehow.

And the more we learn, the more we are wise to the very idea of being wise: We learn that the more we find out, the less we truly know. We learn that while there may be some answers, the questions hold more power and meaning for us. The more we have knowledge, the more we recognize our own ignorance, too.

But to a Study Ninja, curiosity is a wonderful thing. So here's my invitation to you. At every stage of your learning and at every stage in your life, be curious. Be annoyingly curious. About everything. Because indeed every single thing that's pushed the human race forward was born from curiosity. It was born not from a grown-up, sensible person who knew it all; it was born out of a childlike sense of wonder. In an age where the facts are at our fingertips (as soon as the exam is over!), the paradox of learning is this: only from working out what we don't know do we learn new things.

It can sometimes feel like the school process is designed to knock the childishness out of us: we're taught to wear uniforms, arrive on time, do set tasks by certain deadlines. We're told not to play in the dirt or scuff our shoes. Our entire education system seems to be built to prepare humans for workplace conformity rather than to enhance their individuality. But you can still choose to be playful and childish – and

I think this is important, not only for you, but for your learning, and for society as a whole.

The real transition to the global, digital age is yet to come. We are starting to see a devaluing of 'information'. Instead of the six honest serving men of Kipling, these days we can learn pretty much anything in the world with just two trusty companions: YouTube and Google. At the moment, governments seem to have framed the education system around the question of 'what kind of employees do our businesses need?', which I think is limiting in itself, but in answering this question, what's clear is that the higher the frequency and volume of information we receive, the more adaptable and creative we need to become. The idea of a job for life already seems absurd, and as the years go by, we'll place a greater emphasis on our ability to adapt to change, to the extent that whole careers in the same industry will seem equally absurd, and robots replace humans in any job that can be remotely repeatable or automated.

In the future, businesses and societies will reward the innovators, the entrepreneurs, the creatives – the people who ask a lot of questions and seek answers and solutions. It is precisely for this reason that you owe it to yourself to be devilishly curious and childish. Here's a few ways you can do this.

Be comfortable with messy. Reject the perfection brainwashing from school and don't be afraid to do things differently. 'Good enough' beats 'perfect', every time.

Don't be afraid to experiment. If you don't know how to do something, mess about. Play with ideas, try new things. If something doesn't work, you can always tear it up and start again. Nothing ventured, nothing gained.

Stand out, don't blend in. Ignore your lizard brain. True, the old rules say creativity and difference are shame-inducing threats to the status quo. The new rules are that creativity and difference will *become* the status quo. The things that make you stand out are your gifts to the world and it's your duty to share them.

Play. It's one of the most childish things you can do, but some of the most sophisticated ideas in the world have come from playing freely – from beautiful designs to tech solutions to works of art. Muck around, play games, be weird, be silly.

Remember what it is you want to be when you grow up. This will remind you why you chose to learn – because it's always a choice. Stay motivated by recalling what inspired you to start in the first place and the things you're hoping for when you reach the finish line. But above all, enjoy the journey, and gaze out of the window often, because you never know what you might miss.

And finally, do one thing that we tend to not be so good at when we're children: **share**. Share what you learn. Share what you do. Share what you love. Share your curiosities and your sense of wonder with the world. Who else is going to push the human race forward just that tiny bit more, if not you?

I started the book by saying that a Study Ninja is a human, not a superhero. Yes, we all have our faults and flaws, and I'm a big believer that no-one is a guru – not even your favourite teacher – and that everyone has lots still to learn.

But likewise, everyone has something to teach, too. And now you're a Study Ninja, you should make it your duty to teach as well as learn:

to seek out ways to share your knowledge and talents as well as to seek out the ways for others to share their knowledge and talents with you.

If you thought learning finished when you got the certificate, I hope I've changed your mind. And if you were curious before, I hope this book has further fired your curiosity and rekindled that sense of playfulness that will drive you to ask more questions, to ask better questions and to see the world through a childish sense of awe.

If when you go to bed, you realize you understand less of the world than when you got up that morning, then consider that day a success. Because only from curiosity do we truly become enlightened. The world needs your questions as much as it needs your answers and solutions.

So, my Study Ninja, what questions are you going to ask today?

THANK YOUS

A book is never a one-person endeavour, for all sorts of reasons. Thanks to my brilliant editor, Kate Hewson, for making me a better writer as each book goes on, and to the whole team at Icon Books for getting behind this project; Allan Burrell and Emma Brocklesby for making beautiful new Ninja graphics and Marie Doherty for type-setting it so beautifully onto the page; Alex Mason, Holly Standfast and the University of Sussex for your brilliant help with the research; the team at TPHQ for giving me the time, space and confidence to go off and make this, and in particular Elena Boga, Paula Levett and my brilliant assistant, Rachel Bailey; likewise to Chaz and Roscoe for managing without me at home when I was lost in my own little world and to Pearly, Sunil and family from Dreams Cabana, Dalawella, Sri Lanka, where the Ninja mojo slowly returned over sunsets and too much rice and curry.

I'd also like to thank a whole group of people whose feedback helped shape it from 'shitty first draft' to something my lizard brain was finally OK with:

Anna Cox, Rosie Hunham, Matthew Brown, Holly Standfast, Julia Richards, Alex Mason, Grace Marshall, Hayley Watts, Beatrice Atcheson, Jo Walters, Katy Bateson, Nick Wray, Matt Gracie. Thanks also to Talbot's House at Bedford School, especially George Chapman, Dom Blore, Ed Sterling, Philip Gebing, Daniel Lin and Benno Schulz. Your insights, wise counsel and practical ideas were a transformative part of the whole process. Thank you.

Finally, it would be wrong to write a book about learning and not reflect back and thank a few people who have helped me on my own lifelong journey of learning. Mum, Dad and Granny – rest assured I learned as much from the advice I ignored as the advice I followed. Institutions like Lawrence Sheriff School and the University of Birmingham had a profound influence on me, often especially when I was questioning their rigidity or struggling with my Ninja Balance, so special thanks to Rex Pogson, Paddy Wex, Howard Smith, Michael Green (RIP), Stuart Hanson, Frank Webster and Ann Gray for being patient, occasionally critical and always inspirational.

And as the end of the book says, every journey of learning leads to a journey of teaching. So Roscoe, you should know that I've been mainly thinking about you as I've written this book – and not just through hearing your little shrieks and giggles from downstairs. I remember before you were born, your mum telling me you would teach us stuff about ourselves. She was right, as she sometimes is (!). I look forward to being your teacher where you need me to be, and continuing to learn as much from you as I have already.

REFERENCES AND FURTHER READING

Well done for getting all the way to the end of the book! To say thank you, I have put some extra resources online at www.studyninja. online/resources

Chapter 2:

▶ Graham Allcott, *How to be a Productivity Ninja*

Check out Atul Gawande's work here:

▶ Atul Gawande, *The Checklist Manifesto*

▶ Atul Gawande, TED Talk: "How do we heal medicine?"

Other books on productivity and organization:

▶ Stephen Covey, *The Seven Habits of Highly Effective People*

▶ David Allen, *Making It All Work*

Chapter 3:

You can read more about some of the psychological studies referenced here:

▶ http://psycnet.apa.org/psycinfo/2003-02858-014

▶ http://www.psych-it.com.au/Psychlopedia/article.asp?id=385 – Psych-it.com

▶ http://www.sciencedirect.com/science/article/pii/ S0065260110430014 – Advances in Experimental Social Psychology (AESP)

▶ http://www.prismdecision.com/the-planning-fallacy-and-optimism-bias

▶ Stanford Marshmallow Experiment: Mischel, W., Ebbesen, E. B., & Raskoff Zeiss, A. (1972). Cognitive and attentional mechanisms in delay of gratification. *Journal of Personality and Social Psychology*, 21(2), 204.

Chapter 5:

You can read more here:

▶ Highlighting sucks: http://ideas.time.com/2013/01/09/highlighting-is-a-waste-of-time-the-best-and-worst-learning-techniques/

Chapter 6:

There are, unsurprisingly, some fantastic books about writing. My favourites are:

▶ Stephen King, *On Writing*

▶ Natalie Goldberg, *Writing Down the Bones*

Chapter 7:

Dominic O'Brien is a multiple World Memory Champion and Guinness World Record Holder, and his memory techniques are fascinating. You can sample a video here: https://www.youtube.com/watch?v=K1QQ3LdFz18

References:

▶ http://www.psychologytoday.com/blog/ulterior-motives/
  201202/developing-good-study-habits-really-works

▶ Maguire, E. A., Gadian, D. G., Johnsrude, I. S., Good, C.
  D., Ashburner, J., Frackowiak, R. S. J., & Frith, C. D. (2000).
  Navigation-related structural change in the hippocampi of taxi
  drivers. *Proceedings of the National Academy of Sciences of the
  United States of America*, 97(8), 4398–4403.

▶ BDNF in the brain: http://www.ncbi.nlm.nih.gov/pubmed/
  21722657

▶ Heatmaps in the body: Heat map pic: http://www.boston.com/
  dailydose/2013/03/07/ways-exercise-can-boost-your-mental-
  performance/nl4DA55GaKDZbdrAk9EmiO/story.html

▶ Chewing gum: http://changingminds.org/explanations/
  meaning/chewing_thinking.htm

Chapter 8:

The lizard brain analogy and the role of brain functions in procrastination has been covered in various books, including my own *How
to be a Productivity Ninja*. I personally love the following, which offer
slightly different variations on this theme:

▶ Seth Godin, *Linchpin*

▶ Seth's Lizard Brain talk on Vimeo: http://vimeo.com/5895898

▶ Stephen Pressfield, *The War of Art*

▶ Dr Steve Peters, *The Chimp Paradox*

Chapter 9:

References:

▶ Piers Steel study: http://studiemetro.au.dk/fileadmin/www.
studiemetro.au.dk/Procrastination_2.pdf

▶ Kasper: http://www.prweb.com/releases/2004/03/prweb114250.
htm

▶ Baumeister/Tice:

- http://www.psychologicalscience.org/index.php/
publications/observer/2013/april-13/why-wait-the-science-
behind-procrastination.html

- Tice, D. M., & Baumeister, R. F. (1997). Longitudinal study of
procrastination, performance, stress, and health: The costs
and benefits of dawdling. *Psychological Science*, 454–458.

- Ferrari, J. R., & Tice, D. M. (2000). Procrastination as a
self-handicap for men and women: A task-avoidance
strategy in a laboratory setting. *Journal of Research in
Personality*, 34(1), 73–83.

Finally, thank you for reading this book. I'm honoured to have had
your attention, because I know it's the most precious resource
you have. I'd love to hear your story, your top tips to be a Study
Ninja and also how you've found this book. You can email me at
graham@thinkproductive.co.uk – I'd love to hear from you!

Join us on Facebook	Join us on LinkedIn	Follow us on Twitter
Search: Think Productive	Think Productive – The Productivity Ninjas	@grahamallcott @thinkproductive

BRING A PRODUCTIVITY NINJA TO YOUR OFFICE!

If you want to boost productivity in your organization, Think Productive runs a full range of in-house workshops to do exactly that. We started in the UK and are now making our way around the world, too:

GETTING YOUR INBOX TO ZERO

A 3-hour tour through Ninja email tips and tricks, complete with at-desk coaching so that participants finish the workshop with their inboxes actually at zero. Short, practical and dazzlingly effective. Also available as a full-day programme with 'Outlook Ninja'.

'Very satisfying. Love the approach!'
– Julia Ewald, eBay

EMAIL ETIQUETTE

Our Email Etiquette workshop focusses on good and bad email practice and teams leave having written an 'email manifesto' to help improve their email culture. Three hours later, watch the emails in your inbox get easier and easier to deal with as a result.

'Email has always annoyed me! This session brought these issues to the forefront of my mind and we were able to deal with them!'
– Nick Matthews, Cardiff University Students' Union.

STRESS LESS, ACHIEVE MORE

On this full-day workshop, we work both in the classroom and at desks to help people implement Think Productive's CORD workflow model, get their 'second brain' systems set up on computer or paper and fill several recycling bins full of old and useless paperwork. Energizing, clarity-inducing and fun, we regularly have people describe the day as 'life-changing'!

'Very impressed. Actually the most productive and enjoyable course I've ever been on.'
– Lisa Hutchinson, University of Bristol

MAKING MEETINGS MAGIC

A 3-hour workshop designed to transform the world of meetings! We cover good and bad meeting practices, the 40–20–40 continuum and a range of techniques. Coaching and group work focusses on both the individual and team issues with the aim of reducing the time everyone spends in meetings and making the meetings you do attend, well, magic!

> *'Really made us think about using our time*
> *for meetings more productively and in some cases*
> *had us questioning the need for a meeting at all!'*
> *– Alison Jenson, British Airways*

HOW TO BE A PRODUCTIVITY NINJA

Ideal for conferences or team away days, this 1.5-hour talk is centred around the 9 characteristics of the Productivity Ninja as outlined in Graham's bestselling book – and packed full of tips and tricks. It's also a great way to get a taste for our approach and explore which longer workshops might suit you best.

> *'Entertaining and packed with useful ideas.*
> *Extremely useful and thought-provoking.'*
> *– Heath Heatlie, GlaxoSmithKline*

**To find out about bringing our workshops to your company,
email us: hello@thinkproductive.com**

HOW TO BE A STUDY NINJA

Want to continue on your journey to Study Ninja mastery? We've created a dedicated site where you will find:

- Extra articles and exclusive content
- PDF downloads to help with exercises in the book
- Access to online learning and short courses to help make the learning stick

www.studyninja.online

HIRE GRAHAM TO SPEAK

Graham delivers a range of keynote talks and workshops on the productivity of work and learning, all around the world. To find out how to book Graham for your event, visit **www.grahamallcott.com** for more information, or drop us an email: **bookgraham@thinkproductive.co.uk**

CONTACT A PRODUCTIVITY NINJA NEAR YOU

You'll find details of all Think Productive's workshops, webinars and consultancy services on the previous pages and at **www.thinkproductive.com**
Email your nearest Think Productive office:

  UK & Ireland –
hello@thinkproductive.co.uk

Australia –
hello@thinkproductive.com.au

Canada –
hello@thinkproductive.ca

 Netherlands, Belgium & Luxembourg –
hallo@thinkproductive.nl

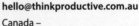 United States –
hello@thinkproductiveusa.com